NorthStar

LISTENING AND SPEAKING
Intermediate

SECOND EDITION

Helen S. Solórzano
Jennifer P. L. Schmidt

Series Editors
Frances Boyd
Carol Numrich

Longman

NorthStar: Listening and Speaking, Intermediate, Second Edition
Teacher's Manual and Achievement Tests

Pearson Education, 10 Bank Street, White Plains, NY 10606

Teacher's Manual by Laurie Barton
Achievement Tests by Tay Lesley

Development director: Penny Laporte
Project manager: Debbie Sistino
Development editors: Mykan White, Bill Preston
Vice president, director of design and production: Rhea Banker
Executive managing editor: Linda Moser
Production editor: Lynn Contrucci
Production manager: Liza Pleva
Production coordinator: Melissa Leyva
Director of manufacturing: Patrice Fraccio
Senior manufacturing buyer: Dave Dickey
Cover design: Rhea Banker
Text design: Quorum Creative Services
Text composition: TSI Graphics
Text font: 11/13 Sabon

ISBN 0-201-78846-2

Printed in the United States of America
4 5 6 7 8 9 10—TCS—09 08 07 06 05 04

Contents

Teacher's Manual

Unit-by-Unit Teaching Suggestions

Achievement Tests

Introduction to the *NorthStar* Series

The *NorthStar* Approach to Language Teaching *NorthStar* is a five-level, integrated skills series for language learning. The series is divided into two strands: listening and speaking, and reading and writing. There are five books in each strand, taking students from the high beginning level of the *Introductory Student Book* to the advanced level of the *Advanced Student Book*. At each level, the two strands explore different aspects of the same contemporary themes. Each book practices language-learning skills through high-interest thematic content.

In addition to the Student Books, the *Writing Activity Book* for each level of the reading and writing strand expands and reinforces the writing process. The *Audio Program* includes, on CD or cassette, all the reading and listening segments as well as pronunciation exercises. The *Video Program* includes 3- to 5-minute segments for each unit. The segments are thematically linked to the units in the Student Books to offer additional material for listening comprehension and discussion or writing.

Integrated skills are at the heart of the *NorthStar* series. When two or more language skills are integrated, language learning is apt to be more authentic, natural, and motivating. Integrating skills offers more opportunity for recycling and reinforcing key vocabulary, grammatical structures, and ideas. As a result, students have more occasions to assimilate information and language, thereby facilitating learning.

Approach to Reading and Writing *NorthStar* supports the approach that learning to be a good writer means learning to be a good reader and vice versa. Reading skills are taught *implicitly* throughout each unit. For example, the comprehension exercises are designed to give practice in reading skills, such as predicting, identifying main ideas and details, skimming and scanning.

Writing skills are taught *implicitly* through the readings: The readings serve as models of good writing. In the Style section, writing skills are taught *explicitly* through analysis, explanation, and guided practice.

The writing process begins at the start of each unit (often with the first Prediction exercise), continues through the unit (with dialogues, written reactions to a partner's comments, chart completion, note taking), includes the Style section (with explicit writing skills and structured practice), and culminates in the Writing Topics section, where students are asked to produce a complete piece of writing.

Reading and writing skills—including strategies for improving vocabulary, comprehension, and grammar—are cultivated in every section of every unit. In the Research Topics section, the reading and writing integration becomes most clear and relevant, as students are asked to conduct research and read texts from a variety of authentic sources and then integrate ideas from these sources into their own writing.

Approach to Listening and Speaking *NorthStar* provides structured opportunities for students to practice listening to many types of discourse. Listening skills are taught *implicitly* throughout each unit. For example, the comprehension exercises are designed to give practice in such listening skills as predicting, identifying main ideas and details, and note taking.

Speaking skills are taught *implicitly* through the listenings: The listenings serve as models of functional language or conventional style. In the Style section, speaking skills are taught *explicitly* though analysis, explanation, a carefully structured pronunciation syllabus, and guided practice. The teaching of speaking begins at the start of each unit (often with the first Prediction exercise), continues through the unit (with categorizing and ranking activities, interviews, games, pronunciation practice, comparing answers and discussing differences, sharing opinions), includes the Style section (with explicit functional skills and structured practice), and culminates in the Speaking Topics section, where students use their speaking skills to create role plays, case studies, debates, radio announcements, and presentations.

Listening and speaking skills—including learning strategies for improving vocabulary, comprehension, and grammar—are cultivated in every section of every unit. In the Research Topics section, the listening and speaking integration becomes most clear and relevant as students are asked to conduct projects such as surveys or in-person and telephone interviews and then integrate ideas from these sources into their own oral presentations.

Approach to Grammar Content drives the organization of the grammar syllabus. Accordingly, students have opportunities to encounter and work with grammar structures in authentic contexts. The purpose of the Grammar section is to enable clear and accurate discussion and writing about the unit theme.

The Grammar section of each unit is not intended to be an exhaustive treatment of a grammatical point. Rather, it is an opportunity for students to focus on a new or familiar point within the specific context of the unit. Teachers and students can use the Grammar section either as the first step in presenting a particular structure or as a review. For more detailed explanations of the grammar points, a chart of Grammar Book References is included in the Student Books. This chart cross-references the unit grammar to appropriate sections in two successful grammar series: Azar's grammar series and *Focus on Grammar*.

Grammar is taught both inductively (through discovery) and deductively (through explanation). First, students answer questions to discover the form, usage, and meaning of the grammar. Next, they read an explanation of the point, with examples in the thematic context of the unit. Finally, students practice the structures in exercises related to the content of the unit.

Approach to Vocabulary Vocabulary practice has been increased in the Second Edition of *NorthStar*. Vocabulary is taught both *directly* and *indirectly*. Specific vocabulary exercises focus on meaning, usage, and word forms. In many of the other exercises (grammar, style, speaking and writing topics, research), the vocabulary reappears but is not the focus of the exercise.

In Section 1, Focus on the Topic, vocabulary has been chosen for its relevance in discussing the topic/theme. In other cases, the vocabulary is essential for comprehension of a listening or reading text, so the focus becomes preteaching vocabulary for comprehension. In Section 3, Focus on Vocabulary, the work takes on a different focus, as words are reviewed and studied in more depth. In this section, students are asked to go beyond the vocabulary presented in the text and explore new items. In the listening and speaking strand, a particular effort has been made to focus on idiomatic and informal expressions that are common in spoken English.

Correction in Oral Work   Students with academic and/or career goals need and want correction. You should listen to what students are saying on two levels: form and content. Use correction to help students close the gap between what they want to say and what they are able to say. Cued self-correction is preferable. Self-correction can be promoted in several ways. You will want to vary your strategies depending on the activity and time available.

- **On-the-spot correction:** As students are talking, you can use a nonverbal gesture (such as raising a finger, pulling an earlobe, writing the error on the board) to indicate that a correction is necessary.

- **Individual notes:** You may want to write down individual student's errors on a chart to have them corrected when the activity is finished. For example, in the Sample Error Chart below, general feedback is on the left-hand side. You can use symbols such as ↑ to mean "above average," → to mean "average," and ↓ to mean "below average." Specific feedback is on the right-hand side. An index card, divided into three equal parts, also works well.

Name _Maria R_ Class _English 101_		
General Feedback Fluency ↑ Accuracy → Pronunciation ↓	**Pronunciation/Stress** *these* /ð/ *think* /θ/	**Grammar/Vocabulary** *Yesterday, they <u>say</u> . . .* *The students work<u>s</u> together . . .*
Notes *Interesting ideas about education.* *Be sure to speak loudly, too.* *Eye contact was much better.*	*ru<u>r</u>al* /ɾ/ *official* *product*	*They have <u>much</u> problems . . .* *They need<u>ed</u> a material subject.*

- **Collective notes:** You may want to take notes that can be used later to create an error-correction exercise.

- **Tapes and transcriptions:** You may want to use tapes and transcriptions to increase students' awareness of language errors. Audiotaping student conversations and reports is especially useful in the pronunciation activities in Sections 4A and 4D, where students have an opportunity for extensive oral production. First, tape the conversation, role play, or report; then record your feedback, modeling correct pronunciation. You can also transcribe a portion for use as an error-correction activity. Use blanks or underscoring to indicate errors; then have students correct their mistakes and encourage them to appreciate how their language is improving. Occasionally, it may be interesting to have students transcribe small bits of their own language for the same purpose.

If possible, you may want to videotape an activity. Play it back and elicit oral and written comments about students' own language and their feelings about seeing themselves speaking English. Follow this with some error correction on the board.

- **Fluency line:** Students need to develop fluency. The following activity develops fluency by giving students a chance to repeat the same story, explanation, or opinion to several different people.

Divide the class in half. Have Group B students line up, side by side, and then have Group A students line up opposite them. Each Group A student then tells the Group B student opposite him or her a story, explanation, or opinion, depending on the assignment. Time the Group A students, giving them a set amount of time to talk. The Group A students must not stop talking, and the Group B students must not interrupt, except to ask for clarification. When you signal, all Group A students must take a step to the right and repeat their comments to their next Group B partner. (The Group A student at the end of the line has to walk around to the far left to find his or her new partner.) The activity continues with you signaling each partner to change. You can speed up the process by incrementally reducing the amount of time between partners. At a designated point, the roles are reversed so that Group B students have an opportunity to talk, and Group A students have an opportunity to listen.

The format of this activity can be modified. For example, you could have students line up in concentric circles instead of lines or have them walk freely around the room, talking with different partners.

- **Audio journal:** An audio journal is like a written journal except that students record their ideas on an audio cassette tape instead of on paper. There are a number of assignments that can lead to audio journals—for example, comments on topics discussed in class, reports on individual research, and first drafts of oral presentations. Some teachers like to have students record pronunciation exercises as a way to individualize error correction. For all these activities, it is important to specify how long the students should speak and whether they should read prepared comments or speak extemporaneously. When you receive the audio journals, you can give students feedback by recording a reply right after their comments. When replying, be sure to discuss both content and form.

A Message from the Series Editors

We think of a good textbook as a musical score or a movie script. It tells you the moves and roughly how quickly and in what sequence to make them. But until you and your students bring it to life, a book is silent and static, a mere possibility. We hope that *NorthStar* orients, guides, and interests you as teachers.

It is our hope that the *NorthStar* series stimulates your students' thinking, which in turn stimulates their language learning, and that they will have many opportunities to reflect on the viewpoints of journalists, commentators, researchers, other students, and people in the community. Further, we hope that *NorthStar* guides them to develop their own point of view on the many and varied themes encompassed by this series.

We welcome your comments and questions. Please send them to us at the publisher:

Frances Boyd and Carol Numrich, Series Editors
NorthStar
Pearson Education
10 Bank Street
White Plains, NY 10606

Overview of the *Teacher's Manual and Achievement Tests*

The *NorthStar Teacher's Manual* includes:

- Specific suggestions for teaching each unit, including:
    - ✓ Unit-by-unit overview (scope and sequence) and summary
    - ✓ Unit-by-unit description of the Focus, Setup, and Expansion/Homework activities for each exercise
    - ✓ Suggested teaching times
    - ✓ Cross-references to the companion strand, Grammar Book References, *Writing Activity Book*, Video, and Companion Website
- The Answer Key to the Student Book
- Reproducible Achievement Tests with Answer Keys—including the test audioscript and test audio CD for the *Listening and Speaking* strand; and a test-generating CD-ROM to allow teachers to customize and adapt the 300 test items and writing tasks on the Reading and Writing Achievement Tests for the *Reading and Writing* strand
- An alphabetized-by-unit word list of the key vocabulary items practiced in each unit

COURSE PLANNER

Each unit contains approximately eight hours of classroom material, plus expansion, homework, and support material. Teachers can customize the units by assigning some exercises for homework and/or eliminating others. To help teachers customize the units for their specific teaching situation, the Unit-by-Unit Teaching Suggestions in the *Teacher's Manual* include 1, 2, or 3 stars to indicate the relative importance of each section or exercise:

✪✪✪ **Essential** sections
✪✪ **Recommended** sections
✪ **Optional** sections

To use *NorthStar* most effectively, see the teaching guide below.

CLASS TIME AVAILABLE PER UNIT	SECTIONS TO COMPLETE
8 hours or more	Essential (✪✪✪), Recommended (✪✪), Optional (✪)
6 hours	Essential (✪✪✪), Recommended (✪✪)
4 hours	Essential (✪✪✪) only

Advertising on the Air

OVERVIEW	
Theme:	Advertising

Listenings:	Listening One: *Advertising on the Air*
	    A classroom lecture
	Listening Two: *Negative Appeals*
	    Another excerpt from the lecture

Critical Thinking Skills:	Critique magazine and television ads Identify salient features of an ad Propose advertising campaigns according to market information Infer word meaning from context Support answers with information from the lecture Identify intended market of ads Compare and contrast advertising strategies Correlate examples with abstract principles
Listening Tasks:	Identify chronology Listen for details Relate listenings to personal values Synthesize information from both listenings Identify emphasis in speech Listen to and evaluate student product promotions Identify message and strategy of student ads
Speaking Tasks:	Make predictions Propose advertising strategy Comment on ads using new vocabulary Read ads aloud with proper stress and intonation Promote a product with attention-grabbing language Offer advice using imperatives Create, rehearse, and perform a TV ad Record a two-minute summary of research
Pronunciation:	Highlighting words
Vocabulary:	Context clues Synonyms Definitions
Grammar:	Imperatives

UNIT SUMMARY

This unit explores the emotional appeals used by advertisers to entice people to buy their products. Listening One is a lecture about the emotional appeals in radio advertising, including examples of radio ads that use different appeals. Listening Two contains more radio ads utilizing negative emotional appeals.

The companion unit of *NorthStar: Reading and Writing* deals with the challenges of advertising products in an international market.

1 Focus on the Topic, PAGE 1

✿✿✿A   PREDICTING

Suggested Time: 5 minutes ⏱

Focus
To get students thinking about the types and strategies of advertising; to examine the meaning of the title and use it to predict the unit content.

Setup
Have students look at the picture and suggest products for question 1. Write the suggestions on the board, and vote on the top three most probable products before doing question 2. While discussing question 3, have students guess the meaning of "on the air" and explain if necessary.

Expansion/Homework
You may want to have student pairs discuss the questions before the class discussion.

✿✿B   SHARING INFORMATION

Suggested Time: 20 minutes 🕐

Focus
To relate the topic of advertising to students' own experiences.

Setup
Have students answer the questions on their own. Then divide the class into groups of four or five (of similar fluency levels, if possible); have students discuss their answers. Then have each group report to the class on the most memorable ad.

Expansion/Homework
To save time, students can answer the questions in groups without working on their own.

Link to *NorthStar: Reading and Writing*
Students using the companion text may want to discuss the following question:
*Would this ad (for Quaker Fruit & Oatmeal) be successful if it were used in
another country?*

✪✪✪ (PREPARING TO LISTEN

BACKGROUND
Suggested Time: 15 minutes 🕐

Focus
To introduce the topic of radio advertising.

Setup
Ask for a volunteer to read the information about radio advertising in the
United States. Then have students work in pairs (of different language
backgrounds, if possible) to answer the question in Exercise 1. Next, try to
reach a consensus on the age group that listens to each station. Then have
students do Exercise 2 in pairs before conducting a whole-group tally of the
stations that are best for advertising each product.

Expansion/Homework
You may want to bring in a few taped radio ads from different types of stations
(classical, rock, news). Have the students listen to the ads and try to identify the
type of station that plays it and which age group listens to the station.

Link to *NorthStar: Reading and Writing*
Students using the companion text might discuss the following questions after
completing Exercise 2: *Think of a country you are familiar with (not the United
States). What are the different types of radio stations? What kinds of products
are advertised on each one?*

VOCABULARY FOR COMPREHENSION
Suggested Time: 15 minutes 🕐

Focus
To introduce advertising vocabulary and concepts to aid comprehension of the
listening.

Setup
Have students pronounce the underlined words. Then pair them up to do the
matching. Go over the answers as a class.

Expansion/Homework
To save time, you can assign the exercise as homework and use class time to
work on pronunciation and to check answers.

2 Focus on Listening, PAGE 5

✪✪✪ A | LISTENING ONE: *Advertising on the Air*

Suggested Time: 5 minutes ⏱

Focus

To encourage students to make predictions about the content of the lecture, and to help students become familiar with the professor's voice.

Setup

Play the introduction and elicit predictions on the content of the lecture. Encourage students to contribute their ideas by calling on several students to make predictions. Affirm each prediction as a possibility.

✪✪✪ LISTENING FOR MAIN IDEAS

Suggested Time: 15 minutes ⏱

Focus

To help students identify the main emotional appeals presented in the lecture; to focus students' attention on the format of the lecture.

Setup

Have students read through Exercises 1 and 2. Explain that Exercise 1 focuses on the main ideas of the lecture, whereas Exercise 2 focuses on how the lecture is presented. Play the lecture once, and have students complete Exercise 1 as they listen. Exercise 2 can be completed at the end of the lecture. Have students compare their answers in pairs (of different listening abilities, if possible) before checking with the class.

✪✪✪ LISTENING FOR DETAILS

Suggested Time: 15 minutes ⏱

Focus

To help students listen for specific details in the lecture.

Setup

Have students read the items and answer the ones they know. Play the lecture, and have students do the rest of the questions. If needed, play the lecture again. Have students work in pairs (of different listening abilities, if possible) to go over the answers. If disagreements arise, replay those segments rather than simply giving the answers.

✪✪ REACTING TO THE LISTENING

Suggested Time: 20 minutes ⏱

Focus

To get students to hypothesize about the audience for the radio ads based on the situations presented, the characters, and the products being sold; to evaluate the effectiveness of different types of appeals.

Setup

Read through the characteristics used to describe markets (gender, age, income, etc.). Play Ad 1 and have students discuss their answers before moving on to Ad 2. During the discussions, make sure that students give reasons for their answers. Emphasize that it's possible for students to have varying opinions as long as their reasoning is sound. In Exercise 2, have students work in pairs (of different language backgrounds, if possible) before discussing the questions as a whole class.

Expansion/Homework

In Exercise 1, you may want to have students discuss Ad 2 in groups (of different listening abilities, if possible) and come to a consensus on the market for the ad. Encourage them to pool ideas in order to expand the chart category labeled "Other." Then have the groups present their audience profiles. Students can read Exercise 2 as homework and prepare to give their answers in class.

✪✪✪B LISTENING TWO: *Negative Appeals*

Suggested Time: 10 minutes ⏱

Focus

To help students identify negative appeals by listening to additional radio advertisements.

Setup

Discuss the negative appeals in the column on the left, and get students to think about examples of ads that use these appeals (e.g., guilt—the use of a crying, uncomfortable baby in an ad for diapers; fear—the sound of a burglar breaking a window in an ad for home alarms). Have the students match each ad to the corresponding appeal. Replay the ads if necessary. Discuss the answers.

✪✪✪C LINKING LISTENINGS ONE AND TWO

Suggested Time: 25 minutes ⏱

Focus

To get students to draw connections between Listenings One and Two; to get students to explore how various appeals fit different types of products.

Setup

Ask students to discuss the questions in pairs or small groups (of different language backgrounds, if possible). Since the answers to question 1 will be subjective, emphasize that the purpose of the groups is for students to clarify and share their opinions rather than to come to a consensus. Have students discuss their answers to question 1 as a class. Have students complete the chart in item 2a in pairs (of different language backgrounds, if possible) and then discuss their ideas with the class. Repeat this procedure for item 2b.

Link to *NorthStar: Reading and Writing*

You can list vocabulary from the *Listening and Speaking* and *Reading and Writing* books on the board and encourage students to use the words during their discussion. Discuss how culture affects the emotional appeals in ads by asking the following questions: (a) *Do advertisements in your culture use appeals to emotion? If so, which emotional appeals do you see most often? If not, why not?* (b) *What differences have you noticed between the emotional appeals used in advertising in the United States and in your culture?* To remind students about the cross-cultural aspects of using emotions in advertising, mention how Japanese TV ads manipulate feelings (Reading One: *Advertising All over the World*). If possible, ask students to bring in an ad from a publication in their native language that they think shows a typical emotional appeal for their culture.

❸ Focus on Vocabulary, PAGE 9

✪ EXERCISE 1
Suggested Time: 10 minutes

Focus
To review new vocabulary words from the lecture.

Setup
Make sure that students understand what a testimonial is. Then have them work in pairs to complete the testimonial. Review the answers as a class.

Expansion/Homework
This exercise can be assigned as homework.

✪ EXERCISE 2
Suggested Time: 20 minutes

Focus
To get students to use the new vocabulary meaningfully in real communication.

Setup
Look at the two ads as a class. Next, model the pronunciation of each question before having students work in pairs (of similar fluency levels, if possible) to discuss the questions. Then call on individual students to share answers with the class.

For extra vocabulary practice, have students work on the self-grading vocabulary activities for the unit on the NorthStar Companion Website at **http://www.longman.com/northstar**.

4 Focus on Speaking, PAGE 11

✪✪A PRONUNCIATION: Highlighting

Suggested Time: 25 minutes ⏱

Focus
To help students identify and produce stress patterns used to highlight important information.

Setup
Read the information about highlighting to the class. Play the excerpt from Listening One. Then read the information about stress patterns to the class. Pair the students up to do Exercise 1. Encourage them to read the dialogue out loud as they circle the highlighted words. Then play the conversations, and have students confirm their choices. Discuss how different stress patterns (pitch, loudness, and length) are used. Have the students work in pairs (of different language backgrounds, if possible) to complete Exercise 2. Review the instructions carefully to make sure they understand their roles as Students A and B. You may want to demonstrate with a student, making sure to give examples of different stress patterns (pitch, loudness, and length).

Expansion/Homework
If time is limited, you can skip the instructions to have students switch ads and read to a different partner.

✪✪✪B STYLE: Attention Grabbers

Suggested Time: 20 minutes ⏱

Focus
To identify and create attention grabbers used to introduce advertisements.

Setup
Read the introductory explanation and the examples of attention grabbers. Have students do Exercise 1 and discuss the answers. For Exercise 2 you may need to write a sample ad before having student pairs write their own ads. Then discuss attention grabbers for each product, calling on students to read their attention grabbers to the class. Make sure students listen to each one carefully so that they can discuss the most interesting attention grabbers.

Link to *NorthStar: Reading and Writing*
You may want to ask students to identify some attention grabbers in Reading Two: *Changing World Markets*. Ask students to discuss how attention grabbers are used in other cultures. Ask them to identify attention grabbers that may work in one culture but not in another.

✪✪ C GRAMMAR: Imperatives

Suggested Time: 20 minutes 🕐

Focus

To practice using imperative forms in preparation for creating an advertisement.

Setup

Read the introductory explanation and the examples of imperatives. Divide the class into two lines as directed. Make sure that students stand and move along the line from classmate to classmate. Call on individual students to share interesting advice with the class before having students switch roles.

Expansion/Homework

(1) You may want to have students add other problems to the list. Encourage them to think of humorous problems that are relevant to their lives. (2) For further practice, offer exercises from *Focus on Grammar, Intermediate*, and *Fundamentals of English Grammar*. See Grammar Book References on page 187 of the Student Book for specific units and chapters.

 For extra listening practice, have students use the NorthStar Companion Video.

✪✪✪ D SPEAKING TOPIC

Suggested Time: 45 minutes 🕐

Focus

To give students a chance to use the information, ideas, vocabulary, and language skills they have acquired from the unit to create their own radio ads.

Setup

Read the directions. Divide students into groups of three (of different language backgrounds and abilities, if possible), explaining that each member should have a speaking part. Encourage students to be creative, and to incorporate appeals and attention grabbers in their ads. Then set deadlines for the completion of each step in the process. After the scripts are written, ask students to mark them for sentence stress before they practice. While groups are performing, have the audience complete the Listening Task on page 17.

Expansion/Homework

You may want to tape-record or videotape the performances so that students can see and hear themselves at a later date. Also, these tapes can highlight areas for future pronunciation work.

Link to *NorthStar: Reading and Writing*

If students are familiar with advertising from the United States, you can have them write two ads for the same product: one targeting people in the United States, and the other targeting people in their culture (both in English). After the performance of the ads, discuss how the ads are different, and why.

✪E RESEARCH TOPICS

LOOKING AT MAGAZINE ADS
Suggested Time: 45 minutes ⏱

Focus
To reinforce the concept of emotional appeals in advertising; to explore magazine ads as a different advertising medium.

Setup
Show some magazine ads and get students to identify the appeals. Ask students to bring in three magazine ads each. Then divide them into groups (of different language backgrounds, if possible) to discuss the questions on page 17. Have each group choose three ads to present to the class.

Expansion/Homework
You may want to add a discussion of magazine versus radio advertising. For example, ask: *What kinds of products are best suited to each medium?* or *What kinds of appeals are best suited to each?*

Link to *NorthStar: Reading and Writing*
You may want to ask students to identify the emotional appeals in the billboard advertisements in their community. *What emotional appeals is the advertiser using? Why is the advertiser using this appeal to sell the product?*

✪ LOOKING AT TV ADS
Suggested Time: 20 minutes ⏱

Focus
To explore TV ads as a different advertising medium; to shift students' focus away from the ads themselves and to the contexts in which they appear.

Setup
Check to see if students have access to televisions and tape recorders. For those who don't, suggest that they contact a classmate who does or inform them of resources nearby. Read the assignment, and distribute a copy of the day's TV program schedule. Discuss the different kinds of shows. Then demonstrate how to prepare an audio journal (see page xiii for description). As a follow-up activity, have students work in groups of four to discuss what they have viewed. Then have them share answers with the class.

Expansion/Homework

Instead of audio journals, you can have students do written journals. In either case, you can have a class discussion on the questions after students have turned in their assignments.

Link to *NorthStar: Reading and Writing*

You can add this question: *In your native country are there as many ads as there are in this country? How are they spaced during programs?* To remind students about when and how often ads appear during programs in different countries, refer students to Reading Two: *Changing World Markets.*

Pushing the Limit

OVERVIEW	
Theme:	Extreme Sports

Listenings:	Listening One: *Journal of a Mountain Climber*
	    An audio journal
	Listening Two: *Sensation Seekers*
	    A psychology lecture

Critical Thinking Skills:	Challenge stereotypes Infer word meaning from context Support opinions with examples from the text Infer information not explicit in the text Correlate an individual example with broad trends Rank outdoor activities Analyze survey results
Listening Tasks:	Identify main ideas Listen for details Interpret speaker's emotions Synthesize information from two listenings Distinguish between vowels sounds Listen for specific information in student responses Classify sounds Listen to student presentations and take notes
Speaking Tasks:	Discuss interests in sports Construct and perform a dialogue using new vocabulary Elaborate extemporaneously on an idea Ask and answer questions about personal preferences Make travel suggestions Express and defend opinions Conduct a survey Present research on a sport
Pronunciation:	Front vowels /iy/, /ɪ/, /ey/, /ɛ/
Vocabulary:	Context clues Definitions Synonyms
Grammar:	Modals of preference

UNIT SUMMARY

This unit explores the personal characteristics of people who enjoy high-risk recreational activities. Listening One is the audio journal of a female mountain climber. Listening Two is a psychology lecture on the traits of people who are sensation seekers.

The companion unit of *NorthStar: Reading and Writing* presents the career of skateboarding champion Tony Hawk and explores the psychological aspects of competitive sports.

1 Focus on the Topic, PAGE 19

✪✪✪ A PREDICTING

Suggested Time: 5 minutes

Focus
To get students thinking about "pushing the limit" in dangerous activities such as mountain climbing and bungee jumping.

Setup
Have students look at the photo and answer the questions in item 1. Then have them read the title and predict the content of the unit by discussing the questions in item 2 with a classmate. Have the pairs share their predictions with the class.

✪✪ B SHARING INFORMATION

Suggested Time: 15 minutes

Focus
To encourage free discussion about personal experiences with dangerous recreational activities.

Setup
Divide the class into small groups (of different fluency levels, if possible). Have them discuss the questions. Then call on individual students to share their experiences with the whole class.

Expansion/Homework
You may have some students in your class who have not participated in such activities. In this case, you can ask them to explain whether they would if they had the opportunity. Try to elicit reasons for and against participation in high-risk recreation.

✪✪✪ C PREPARING TO LISTEN

BACKGROUND
Suggested Time: 15 minutes

Focus
To introduce the topic of extreme sports and to consider what types of people participate in them.

Setup
Have students complete the exercise in small groups (of different fluency levels, if possible). Then have them share their descriptions with the class. If disagreement arises, encourage discussion. Be sure to have them explain whether the information on page 20 surprises them.

Expansion/Homework
Ask students if they know anyone who participates in extreme sports. A possible question might be, *Is this person similar to the people described in the book?*

VOCABULARY FOR COMPREHENSION
Suggested Time: 15 minutes

Focus
To introduce vocabulary and concepts related to mountain climbing in preparation for the listening.

Setup
Have students read the sentences and select definitions individually before exchanging books and checking each other's answers. Go over the answers, and practice the pronunciation of the underlined words with the class.

Expansion/Homework
To save time, you can assign the exercise as homework and use class time to work on pronunciation and check answers.

2 Focus on Listening, PAGE 22

✪✪✪ A LISTENING ONE: *Journal of a Mountain Climber*

Suggested Time: 5 minutes

Focus
To introduce mountain climber Jennifer Ulman and her audio journal; to identify where she is on Mt. Shasta, and to become familiar with her voice.

Setup

Look at the illustration and read the instructions beneath it. Play the excerpt, and have students guess Jennifer's location. Affirm each guess as a possibility.

✪✪✪ LISTENING FOR MAIN IDEAS
Suggested Time: 10 minutes ⏱

Focus

To help students understand the main ideas in the audio journal.

Setup

Have students read the statements. Play the audio journal one time without stopping. Have students mark the statements true or false while they listen. After listening, have students compare their answers in pairs (of different listening abilities, if possible) before checking them as a class.

✪✪✪ LISTENING FOR DETAILS
Suggested Time: 15 minutes ⏱

Focus

To help students listen for specific details in the audio journal.

Setup

Have students read the items and answer the ones they know. Play the audio journal, and have students complete the sentences. If needed, play the audio journal one more time. Go over the answers. If disagreements arise, replay those segments rather than simply giving the answers.

✪✪ REACTING TO THE LISTENING
Suggested Time: 20 minutes ⏱

Focus

To help students understand the speaker's feelings and how they are expressed vocally.

Setup:

Read the instructions, and make sure students understand how to complete the chart. Stop after each excerpt, and go over the answers. Allow disagreement if it arises. Do Exercise 2 as a class, making sure that the students use examples from the listening to answer question 1. Encourage free discussion of question 2.

Expansion/Homework

You may want to have students meet in groups (of different listening abilities, if possible) to discuss their completion of the chart. Then you can have each group give their explanation of one excerpt. Students can also do the discussion questions in groups (of different fluency levels, if possible).

✪✪✪ B   ## LISTENING TWO: *Sensation Seekers*

Suggested Time: 10 minutes ⏱

Focus
To present psychological concepts related to high-risk recreation.

Setup
Read the introductory statement, and play the lecture. Have students complete the statements as they listen. Then have students compare answers with a classmate.

✪✪✪ C   ## LINKING LISTENINGS ONE AND TWO

Suggested Time: 20 minutes ⏱

Focus
To use the psychological concepts presented in Listening Two in thinking critically about the mountain climber in Listening One.

Setup
Give students time to think about the questions in Exercise 1 and jot down notes before meeting in groups (of different language backgrounds, if possible). Assign group leaders to call on each group member and lead a discussion. After the groups finish, discuss the questions as a class. Then have students work in the same groups to complete the chart in Exercise 2. Compare answers as a class.

Link to *NorthStar: Reading and Writing*
(1) Students can apply the information from Listening Two in discussing the personality traits of skateboarder Tony Hawk (Reading One: *An Interview with Tony Hawk*). (2) They can interview a classmate to find out whether the classmate is a sensation seeker. Possible questions include: (a) *Do you like rock music? Do you like horror movies? Why or why not?* (b) *Would you like to start a new business? Would you like to work as an emergency room doctor? Why or why not?* (c) *Do you get bored doing the same thing every day? Why or why not?* After the interviews, students can present information to the class. You can keep a tally on the board to identify how many students in the class are sensation seekers.

3 Focus on Vocabulary, PAGE 26

❖ **EXERCISE 1**
Suggested Time: 15 minutes ⏱

Focus
To review new vocabulary from the unit.

Setup

Read the instructions, and model the pronunciation of the words in the boxes. Have students complete the journal entries in pairs. Then call on volunteers to read a paragraph from each journal entry to the class.

Expansion/Homework

This exercise can be done as homework and reviewed in class.

✪ EXERCISE 2
Suggested Time: 40 minutes ⏱

Focus

To use the new vocabulary to create an original dialogue.

Setup

Read the instructions and introductory example. Have students work with a partner (from a different language background, if possible). Set a time limit for preparation, and circulate among pairs, offering help if needed. As they practice, encourage students to vary their speaking volume and speed.

Expansion/Homework

Students can prepare the dialogues as homework, if their schedules allow them to meet outside of class. If you have a large class, you can schedule performances on two separate dates to avoid using too much class time at once.

 For extra vocabulary practice, have students work on the self-grading vocabulary activities for the unit on the NorthStar Companion Website at **http://www.longman.com/northstar**.

▌4 **Focus on Speaking,** PAGE 28

✪✪ A   PRONUNCIATION: Front Vowels /iy/, /ɪ/, /ey/, and /ɛ/
Suggested Time: 25 minutes ⏱

Focus

To practice the pronunciation of front vowels in the context of Listenings One and Two.

Setup

Read the introductory chart, and play the audio so students can hear the pronunciation of the front vowels. Play the audio for Exercise 1, and make sure that students are pronouncing both words in each set. Then play the audio for Exercise 2, and go over the answers. Read the instructions for Exercise 3, and pair students with a classmate. Play the audio for Exercise 4, and have students check their answers with their partner. Circulate among pairs, and monitor their pronunciation of the phrases.

Expansion/Homework

You can play a game by dividing the class into teams. Write each of the front vowel symbols on the board, and award one point for every word they can think of that corresponds with each symbol. Write each word on the board, and encourage them to think of as many words as possible. At the end, the team with the most points wins.

✪✪✪B   **STYLE: Giving Reasons and Elaborating**

Suggested Time: 20 minutes 🕙

Focus

To practice giving reasons for ideas and opinions.

Setup

Read the introduction and examples. Make sure students understand that they must follow all three steps in the exercise when giving their answers. Have them work in small groups (of similar fluency levels, if possible). Appoint a leader to keep the process flowing smoothly. After they have finished, call on each group to share an answer with the class.

Expansion/Homework

These questions can be assigned as speaking topics for students to prepare at home. To provide variety, you can assign the questions rather than allow students to choose one themselves. Make sure that students include three parts in their speeches: (1) an idea or opinion; (2) reasons; and (3) elaboration (details).

✪✪C   **GRAMMAR: Modals of Preference**

Suggested Time: 25 minutes 🕙

Focus

To practice using modals of preference in preparation for the speaking topic.

Setup

Call on volunteers to read the dialogue in Exercise 1. Then read the explanatory chart. Make sure that students understand the difference between *to* used in the infinitive and *to* used in comparisons. Read the instructions for Exercise 2. Have students work with a partner (of a different language background, if possible). Circulate among pairs as they complete the questions and think of adventure trips for each other. Call on a few students to share their adventure trip ideas with the class. Discuss whether or not these trips would be enjoyable for the students' partners.

Expansion/Homework

(1) You may want to do this as a role-play activity. After students have completed the questions and discussed their adventure trip ideas, have them play the roles of travel agent and client. One way to begin the role play is as follows:

AGENT: I have a wonderful adventure trip for you.
CLIENT: Really? What is it?

In the role play, make sure that the client responds with a clear preference for either accepting or declining the trip. Have all students practice the role play, and then call on a few volunteer pairs to perform for the class. (2) For further practice, offer exercises from *Focus on Grammar, Intermediate*, and *Fundamentals of English Grammar*. See Grammar Book References on page 187 of the Student Book for specific units and chapters.

 For extra listening practice, have students use the NorthStar Companion Video.

✪✪✪ D SPEAKING TOPIC

Suggested Time: 25 minutes

Focus

To give students a chance to use the knowledge, vocabulary, and skills they have acquired from the unit to discuss high-risk recreational activities.

Setup

Place students in small groups (of similar fluency, if possible). Then read the instructions for Exercise 1. Circulate among the groups, and make sure that they are taking notes and using language from Sections 4B and 4C. Appoint a group spokesperson to take notes on the group discussion in preparation for Exercise 2. As a class, discuss the questions in Exercise 2, with each spokesperson representing his or her group.

Expansion/Homework

(1) Have the students add their own ideas to the list of activities. (2) As a follow-up activity, have students research activities that are available in their local areas and present information to the class on scheduling and prices.

✪✪ E RESEARCH TOPICS

EXTREME SPORTS SURVEY
Suggested Time: 25 minutes

Focus

To encourage students to find out more about high-risk recreational activities by interviewing people who are involved in difficult and dangerous sports.

Setup

Help students identify people they can interview for the survey. Explain the survey instructions, and have students complete the survey individually before pooling information in small groups (of different language backgrounds, if possible). Appoint a group leader to oversee the analysis of survey data. Then have each group report its survey findings to the class.

Expansion/Homework

Students can conduct the surveys in their native languages if necessary, and then report the results in English. In this case, the reporting portion of the exercise is more important.

RESEARCH ON EXTREME SPORTS
Suggested Time: 25 minutes 🕐

Focus

To give students a chance to learn more about a sport of their choice.

Setup

Read the instructions, and give some general guidelines for the short presentations. Make sure that students take notes while listening to the presentations so that they can explain their preferences.

Expansion/Homework

If students have access to PowerPoint technology, they can use it to enhance their presentations. Another option is to have them create educational posters about extreme sports. Give guidelines on length and layout, and ask students to include illustrations, charts, and diagrams. Posters can then be displayed on the classroom walls.

Too Good to Be True

OVERVIEW

Theme:	Fraud

Listenings:	Listening One: *Too Good to Be True*
	    A news report on fraud
	Listening Two: *Interviews*
	        Four interviews with victims of fraud

Critical Thinking Skills:	Critique a solicitation from a con artist Theorize about the success of fraud Infer word meaning from context Support opinions with reasons Evaluate one's susceptibility to fraud Choose appropriate punishments for criminal acts Hypothesize outcomes
Listening Tasks:	Identify chronology in a report Listen for details Interpret speaker's tone and emotions Support answers with information from the text Identify a con artist's strategies Listen for rhythm in speech Listen for reductions in speech View and critique a movie Listen to and comment on student research findings
Speaking Tasks:	Describe types of fraud Share experiences Make predictions Recount experiences using new vocabulary Express and defend opinions Facilitate a group discussion Agree or disagree with statements Make comparative statements Present research findings on fraud
Pronunciation:	Reductions
Vocabulary:	Context clues Definitions
Grammar:	Equatives and comparatives

UNIT SUMMARY

This unit explores the psychology behind fraud: the steps a con artist takes to manipulate a victim and why people become victims of fraud. Listening One is a news report that includes a telephone conversation between a con artist and his victim. Listening Two contains statements from different victims of telephone fraud who explain why they fell for the fraud.

The companion unit of *NorthStar: Reading and Writing* deals with medical quackery and fraudulent health-care products.

1 Focus on the Topic, PAGE 37

✪✪✪A PREDICTING

Suggested Time: 5 minutes ⏱

Focus
To get students thinking about a specific case of fraud.

Setup
After students read the letter and the title, elicit responses to the questions. Write the responses for question 1 on the board: buy something, call somebody, tour real estate, give personal information, send money, etc. Then ask the students to explain what they think the title means.

Expansion/Homework
You may want students to work in pairs (of different language backgrounds, if possible) to brainstorm, and then report their ideas to the class.

✪✪B SHARING INFORMATION

Suggested Time: 20 minutes 🕐

Focus
To encourage free discussion of types of fraud and students' experiences with fraud.

Setup
After students complete Exercise 1, ask for a description of sweepstakes fraud (e.g., when a game of chance promises big prizes, but just takes your money). Then divide the class into groups of three or four, and have them come up with descriptions of the other kinds of fraud. Have students add to the list, and then have one student from each group report (Exercise 2).

Expansion/Homework
For Exercise 1, you may want to divide the types of fraud among the groups, and have each group report to the class while the other students take notes. Then the whole class can add to the list and share their experiences (Exercise 2).

Link to *NorthStar: Reading and Writing*
You can add health product fraud to the list of kinds of fraud in Exercise 1 in the *Listening and Speaking* book. Ask students to write a description of it.

✪✪✪ C PREPARING TO LISTEN

BACKGROUND
Suggested Time: 15 minutes ⏱

Focus
To familiarize students with the crime of telemarketing fraud.

Setup
Read the paragraph on telemarketing fraud, and then ask for student volunteers to read the Fraud Facts chart. Discuss the questions with the whole class, calling on several students for their ideas. Ask them if they have any experience with telemarketing fraud.

Expansion/Homework
You may want to use the Fraud Facts chart as a dictation exercise. Have the students close their books and write down the facts that you read out loud. Next, they can look at the chart to check what they have written. Or you can assign this entire section as homework, using class time to discuss the questions.

Link to *NorthStar: Reading and Writing*
You can ask students to compare the crime of telemarketing fraud to that of medical quackery in the *Reading and Writing* book.

VOCABULARY FOR COMPREHENSION
Suggested Time: 15 minutes ⏱

Focus
To introduce vocabulary and concepts related to fraud to aid comprehension of the listening.

Setup
Have students complete the exercise individually before comparing their answers with a partner. Practice the pronunciation of the underlined words with the class, and then go over the answers.

Expansion/Homework
You may want to assign the exercise as homework, using class time to work on pronunciation and check answers. Another option is to read the letter to the students and have them complete the exercise with a classmate. Encourage discussion afterward with questions such as *Have you ever received a letter like this?* or *Have you ever been offered a vacation?*

✌ **Focus on Listening,** PAGE 41

✪✪✪ A | LISTENING ONE: *Too Good to Be True*

Suggested Time: 5 minutes 🕐

Focus
To encourage students to make predictions about what will happen during the telephone call between Frank and Suzanne; to identify the voices of the reporter, Nadine Chow, the con artist, Frank Richland, and the victim, Suzanne Markham.

Setup
Have students read the questions, then listen to the beginning of the news reports and discuss the questions as a class. Elicit several ideas for question 2 using the vocabulary from Section 1C: *She'll be a victim of fraud; she'll send a deposit and lose it to the con artist, etc.*

✪✪✪ LISTENING FOR MAIN IDEAS
Suggested Time: 10 minutes 🕐

Focus
To help students listen for the main ideas in the news report.

Setup
Have students read the statements and then number them as they listen. Play the audio once only. Have students compare their answers in pairs (of different fluency levels, if possible) and check them as a class.

✪✪✪ LISTENING FOR DETAILS
Suggested Time: 15 minutes 🕐

Focus
To help students listen for specific details in the news report.

Setup
First have students read the items, answering the ones they already know. Play the news report again, and have students complete the statements. If needed, play the conversation again. Go over the answers. If disagreements arise, replay those segments rather than simply giving the answers.

✪✪ REACTING TO THE LISTENING
Suggested Time: 20 minutes 🕐

Focus
To encourage students to make inferences about the fraud victim's feelings based on tone of voice and word choice.

Setup

Read the list of emotions, and make sure students understand each one. Play Excerpt 1, and allow time for students to choose the appropriate emotion. Check their answers before moving on to Excerpts 2–5. Make sure that they give reasons for their choices. Help students focus on how Suzanne speaks rather than simply on what she says. Call on several students to answer the questions in Exercise 2. Elicit a variety of answers.

Expansion/Homework

You can read the questions in Exercise 2 and then have the students work in pairs (of different language backgrounds, if possible). To encourage discussion, you might ask the following questions: *Have you ever been swindled by phone? Has anyone ever called you and asked you to send money? Do you have any friends or family members who are gullible?* If students have "gullible" stories, you may want to divide them into groups, one storyteller each, then have the storytellers move from group to group to retell how they were swindled, allowing them to steadily improve their storytelling as they go.

✪✪✪ B ▐ LISTENING TWO: *Interviews*

Suggested Time: 15 minutes ⏱

Focus

To extend students' understanding of the psychology of fraud by listening to several victims talk about their experience.

Setup

Read the introduction and then have students read the victims' names and reasons for trusting Frank. Then play the audio, and have them match the victim to the reason. Invite students to check their answers with a partner. Go over the answers, replaying problematic segments.

✪✪✪ C ▐ LINKING LISTENINGS ONE AND TWO

Suggested Time: 15 minutes ⏱

Focus

To get students to reflect on the fraud victims' experiences and feelings; to apply the ideas and language to broader questions about the students' experience and human nature.

Setup

Divide students into groups of three (of similar fluency levels, if possible) to discuss the questions and complete the chart for item 2. Then have them report highlights of the discussion to the class. Or work with the whole class, getting students to listen to and respond to one another's ideas. Encourage the use of vocabulary from Section 1C by listing it on the board and referring students to it. Correct pronunciation and usage errors.

Link to *NorthStar: Reading and Writing*

You can list vocabulary from both books on the board and encourage students to use the words during their discussion. Ask students to discuss the following questions: *Quack medicine is a common type of fraud. What are some examples of quack medicine? Have you ever had an experience with quackery?* To remind students about quack medicine, refer to Reading One: *A Miracle Cure?*

❸ Focus on Vocabulary, PAGE 45

✪ EXERCISE 1
Suggested Time: 10 minutes

Focus
To review vocabulary items from the unit.

Setup
Model the pronunciation of target words for students to repeat. Then have them complete the sentences individually. Review the answers as a class.

Expansion/Homework
This exercise can be assigned as homework.

✪ EXERCISE 2
Suggested Time: 15 minutes

Focus
To give students an opportunity to use new vocabulary creatively.

Setup
Have students work with a partner (of a different language background, if possible). Model the pronunciation of target words, and provide an example story, following the suggested beginning. Encourage students to be humorous and/or dramatic and to use as many target words as possible. Circulate among pairs as they tell stories, monitoring the use of target words. Choose two or three interesting stories to have students share with the class.

Expansion/Homework
You can have students dictate stories for you to write on the board. Underline target vocabulary words.

For extra vocabulary practice, have students work on the self-grading vocabulary activities for the unit on the NorthStar Companion Website at **http://www.longman.com/northstar**.

4 Focus on Speaking, PAGE 47

✪✪ A PRONUNCIATION: Reductions

Suggested Time: 20 minutes 🕐

Focus
To help students understand and practice common reductions as they use vocabulary from the unit in a pronunciation chant.

Setup
Begin by writing the following question on the board: *Are you going to send the deposit?* Next, have students repeat it after you. Ask students how they pronounced *going to*, and write their phonetic explanations on the board. Explain reductions, and then have students open their books and study the chart, noting the differences between written and spoken English. For Exercise 1, say or play the chant while students listen. Next, say the chant, and have students repeat after you. Then have them repeat the chant in pairs and then in two large groups. Lead each group, speeding up as you go. In Exercise 2, have students read the dialogue silently and underline the phrases that can be reduced. Next, discuss answers in pairs or as a class. Then have pairs of students read the dialogue out loud, using reductions. Explain that these spoken forms are commonly used by educated speakers in everyday speech. Mention that these forms should not be used in writing.

Expansion/Homework
You can have students record the chant individually in an audio journal entry (see page xiii for instructions). Listen to the recordings, and then record your feedback, modeling corrections for them on the tape.

✪✪✪ B STYLE: Expressing and Asking for Opinions

Suggested Time: 20 minutes 🕐

Focus
To help students express and ask for opinions on the subject of fraud victims and perpetrators, a function that will be used again in the final speaking activity of the unit.

Setup
Elicit phrases for expressing and asking for opinions, and write them on the board. Have students open their books and read the introductory statement and the phrases in the box. Have them write down phrases from the board that don't appear in the box. Divide the students into groups (of different language abilities, if possible) and appoint group leaders for Exercise 1. Have one group read the model. Encourage everyone to use phrases and to express authentic opinions as they do Exercise 2. Monitor the group work, and remind students to use the phrases as necessary.

Expansion/Homework
To encourage students to use the target phrases to express and ask for opinions, you may also want to have a student in each group count how many times the other students use these phrases during the discussion.

✪✪C GRAMMAR: Equatives and Comparatives

Suggested Time: 15 minutes 🕐

Focus
To have students practice using equatives and comparatives in preparation for the final speaking activity of the unit.

Setup
In Exercise 1, read the introduction, and then have two students read the dialogue out loud. Discuss the questions as a whole class. Next, read the information in the grammar chart. For Exercise 2, have two students read the example so that the roles are clear. Give an example of disagreement (e.g., *I don't agree because violent criminals are more unusual than con artists*). Then divide students into pairs (of similar fluency levels, if possible) to do the exercise. Circulate among pairs and correct their errors as needed. You may want to write a few common errors on the board for the whole class to correct. Remind the students to change roles after item 4.

Expansion/Homework
(1) For Exercise 2, you can divide the class into two groups (A and B) standing in lines opposite each other. Group A students move down the line and say each statement three times, to three different Group B students. Group B students listen to each statement, agree or disagree, and tell why. After statement 4, the groups switch roles and repeat the activity. (2) To check your students' grammatical usage, you can ask them to complete Exercise 2 in writing for homework (after they have done the exercise in class). Then collect the papers, and make corrections. (3) For further practice, offer exercises from *Focus on Grammar, Intermediate*, and *Fundamentals of English Grammar*. See Grammar Book References on page 187 of the Student Book for specific units and chapters.

 For extra listening practice, have students use the NorthStar Companion Video.

✪✪✪ D ▎ SPEAKING TOPIC

Suggested Time: 30 minutes 🕐

Focus

To give students a chance to use the knowledge, vocabulary, and skills they have acquired from the unit; to have a higher-level discussion on fraud than was previously possible.

Setup

Divide the class into groups of three or four (preferably students who work well together). Read the list of actions, and have the students decide on a punishment for each one. Encourage them to think of other punishments. If there are disagreements about particular punishments, have the groups vote to achieve consensus. Emphasize that the point of the section is to practice comparing and expressing opinions. The students should not be concerned about finding the "right" answer. Circulate among groups to monitor students' use of the grammar and functional language from the unit. Summarize the ideas on the board as a class. Ask students to explain their rationale for choosing each punishment.

Expansion/Homework

You can assign this exercise as homework and use class time for discussion.

Link to *NorthStar: Reading and Writing*

You can mention that action 4 is an example of health fraud. You can also add the following item to the list of dishonest activities: *Selling a health product that doesn't work.*

✪ E ▎ RESEARCH TOPICS

WATCH A MOVIE

Suggested Time: 2 hours for movie; 25 minutes for discussion 🕐

Focus

To help students use their new understanding of fraud victims and perpetrators to analyze a popular movie.

Setup

Preview the movie you choose. Have students read the questions first. Show the film in class or during lab hours. You may also choose to go to a movie theater to view a current film dealing with fraud. Follow up with small-group discussion and reports by students on particular questions.

Expansion/Homework

(1) After the discussions you can have students record a summary of the movie in their audio journals. In their summaries, they should focus on fraud—how someone took something from somebody by telling a lie. (2) You may want to write down snippets of movie dialogue that contain idiomatic expressions and useful vocabulary related to crime or fraud. Then help students use the context to guess the meaning. (3) If your class time is limited, you may want to limit the movie viewing to key scenes that clearly convey the idea of fraud.

RESEARCH ON FRAUD
Suggested Time: 25 minutes

Focus

To help students find out about other fraudulent activities by doing library or Internet research.

Setup

Have students work alone or in pairs (of students who work well together). Remind them to look for the specific information and to add interesting details that they discover. Encourage them to bring in any questions they have—about vocabulary, concepts, and cultural mores—as they do the research. Then have students create posters to present their research. You may want to prepare a simple worksheet for students to use during the Listening Task. After the presentations, work as a class to develop a list of general rules for protection against fraud. You may have a student volunteer create a poster listing these rules to be posted on a class bulletin board, along with some of the most eye-catching fraud posters.

Expansion/Homework

You might want to have students ask questions of a law-enforcement official, lawyer, or campus security official while doing their research. Similarly, you can find someone to speak to the group about common fraudulent activities and what students can do to protect themselves.

Link to *NorthStar: Reading and Writing*

You can encourage some students to do their research on health-care fraud topics.

The Art of Storytelling

OVERVIEW

Theme:	Storytelling

Listenings:	Listening One: "Lavender"
	    A story
	Listening Two: *An Interview with Jackie Torrence*
	    A conversation with a professional storyteller

Critical Thinking Skills:	Interpret a photograph Express opinions about different types of storytelling Infer word meaning from context Analyze storytelling techniques Analyze and describe characters in a story Support opinions with reasons Match actions to their consequences Interpret meaning from text
Listening Tasks:	Listen for the main ideas Identify chronology in the story Interpret a speaker's emotions Synthesize information from two listenings Take a dictation Identify stress patterns in speech Listen for specific information in student responses Take notes on interviewee responses Listen to and evaluate student responses
Speaking Tasks:	Make predictions Enhance storytelling with adjectives, adverbs, and details Practice composing descriptive sentences Make statements of purpose Collaborate to create, rehearse, and perform a story Record a summary of a story Conduct an interview
Pronunciation:	Rhythm of prepositional phrases
Vocabulary:	Context clues Word definitions Synonyms Dictionary work
Grammar:	Infinitives of purpose

UNIT SUMMARY

This unit explores the art of storytelling. Listening One is "Lavender," a story told by professional storyteller Jackie Torrence. Listening Two is an interview with Ms. Torrence.

The companion unit of *NorthStar: Reading and Writing* presents the story "The Metamorphosis," written by Franz Kafka.

1 Focus on the Topic, PAGE 55

✪✪✪A PREDICTING

Suggested Time: 5 minutes

Focus
To get students to consider the art of storytelling by comparing it to other art forms.

Setup
Have students look at the picture and describe what is happening. Discuss the title, asking students to compare storytelling with other arts.

Expansion/Homework
You may want to have students jot down answers to the questions and compare them with a classmate before the class discussion.

✪✪B SHARING INFORMATION

Suggested Time: 20 minutes

Focus
To encourage free discussion about the students' own experiences with storytelling; to compare storytelling to other forms of entertainment.

Setup
Read through the discussion questions. Have students work in pairs (of different fluency levels, if possible) to discuss them. Then write the three types of entertainment on the board, and call on each pair to discuss their favorite type. Keep a tally on the board to present class preferences. Elicit a few specific titles of each type of story.

Link to *NorthStar: Reading and Writing*
You can help prepare students for Kafka's "The Metamorphosis" by asking the following questions: *Do you like true stories or imaginary stories? When you were a child, did you like stories about animals? Which ones did you like? Do you enjoy horror stories? Why or why not?*

✪✪✪ C **PREPARING TO LISTEN**

BACKGROUND
Suggested Time: 20 minutes 🕐

Focus
To familiarize students with the biography of storyteller Jackie Torrence.

Setup
Read the biography to the class. Then have the students answer the questions in pairs. Go over the answers together.

Expansion/Homework
(1) You can assign this activity as homework, using class time to discuss the questions. (2) You can have the students describe other characteristics of a good storyteller, such as imagination, humor, and use of props and sound effects.

VOCABULARY FOR COMPREHENSION
Suggested Time: 10 minutes 🕐

Focus
To introduce vocabulary items that students will encounter in Listening One.

Setup
Have students read the sentences in Exercise 1 and select synonyms from the list. Model the pronunciation of each synonym as it is chosen. Next, model the pronunciation of the words (items 1–6) in Exercise 2 and have students write each letter next to the corresponding word.

Expansion/Homework
To save time, you can assign the exercises as homework and use class time to work on pronunciation and check answers.

2 Focus on Listening, PAGE 59

✪✪✪ A **LISTENING ONE: "Lavender"**
Suggested Time: 5 minutes 🕐

Focus
To encourage students to make predictions about the story; to become familiar with the voice of the storyteller.

Setup
Before they listen to the excerpt, have students read the prediction questions. Then play the excerpt, and ask them to explain their predictions. Affirm each prediction as a possibility.

✪✪✪ LISTENING FOR MAIN IDEAS
Suggested Time: 10 minutes ⏱

Focus
To help students identify the main ideas of the story.

Setup
Allow students to read the questions, then play the story once. Have students jot down their answers while listening and then compare their answers in pairs. Go over the answers as a class.

✪✪✪ LISTENING FOR DETAILS
Suggested Time: 15 minutes ⏱

Focus
To help students put events from the story in order.

Setup
Have students read the events and see if they can place any of them in the correct order. Next, play the story again all the way through, and have students complete the ordering task. Then have them check their answers with a classmate. Go over the answers. If disagreements arise, replay those segments rather than simply giving the answers.

✪✪ REACTING TO THE LISTENING
Suggested Time: 15 minutes ⏱

Focus
To help students make inferences about the emotions of characters in the story; to identify the techniques used by the storyteller to convey emotions.

Setup
Read the instructions, and give an example of each technique to make sure that students understand it. Play each excerpt, and have the students complete the chart individually while listening. Replay the excerpts as needed. Then have the students compare their answers in small groups (of different listening abilities, if possible). Go over the answers, then have the same groups discuss the questions in Exercise 3. Call on individual students to share their answers with the class.

Expansion/Homework
You can ask the students if "Lavender" reminds them of any stories they know from their home cultures. If students have other stories to share, you may want to divide them into groups with one storyteller each. Then have the storytellers move from group to group to retell the story, allowing them to steadily improve their storytelling as they go.

Link to *NorthStar: Reading and Writing*
You can bring "The Metamorphosis" into the discussion of "Lavender." Use the questions in Exercise 3 to analyze "The Metamorphosis," and then ask the students to explain which story they enjoyed more.

✪✪✪ B **LISTENING TWO: *An Interview with Jackie Torrence***

Suggested Time: 20 minutes 🕐

Focus

To help students understand the steps that Jackie Torrence takes when she tells a story.

Setup

Read the instructions. Play the interview while students complete the matching activity in Exercise 1. Go over the answers. Next, call on individual students to answer the questions in Exercises 2 and 3. Elicit a variety of answers. If students are having difficulty, replay parts of the interview as needed.

Expansion/Homework

Students can complete the questions in Exercises 2 and 3 in pairs (of different listening abilities, if possible). Then you can call on pairs to share their answers with the class.

✪✪✪ C **LINKING LISTENINGS ONE AND TWO**

Suggested Time: 15 minutes 🕐

Focus

To get students to identify the personality that the storyteller creates for each character and to draw inferences about the storyteller's personality.

Setup

Give students time to think about the questions and jot down notes before meeting in pairs (of different fluency levels, if possible). Call on several pairs to share their ideas. Write adjectives on the board in response to the questions. Explain the meaning of adjectives if necessary.

Expansion/Homework

To save time, you can assign one personality—David, Robert, Lavender, or Jackie Torrence—to each pair.

Link to *NorthStar: Reading and Writing*

Students can use adjectives to describe the personalities of characters in "The Metamorphosis." They can also describe the personality of the author, Franz Kafka.

3 Focus on Vocabulary, PAGE 63

✪ EXERCISE 1

Suggested Time: 15 minutes 🕐

Focus

To review vocabulary items from the story.

Setup

Read the instructions, and make sure the students understand how to unscramble the letters. Have the students complete this exercise individually, and then go over the answers.

Expansion/Homework

This exercise can be done as homework.

✪ EXERCISE 2

Suggested Time: 20 minutes 🕘

Focus

To give the students a chance to use the new vocabulary in retelling the story from Listening One.

Setup

Read the instructions, and write some key vocabulary items on the board. Make sure that the students understand that they must use the past tense. You might want to do Picture 1 as an example for the class to follow. Have students complete this activity in pairs (of different language backgrounds, if possible). Circulate among pairs, making sure that students are using as much target vocabulary as possible.

Expansion/Homework

After having the students complete this activity in pairs, you can play a game. Divide the class into two teams. Call on individual students from each team to create a sentence describing each picture. Award one point for every sentence that includes target vocabulary and is clearly related to the story. Do not call on any individual more than once. This will encourage as many students as possible to participate.

 For extra vocabulary practice, have students work on the self-grading vocabulary activities for the unit on the NorthStar Companion Website at **http://www.longman.com/northstar**.

4 Focus on Speaking, PAGE 65

✪✪ A   PRONUNCIATION: Rhythm of Prepositional Phrases

Suggested Time: 20 minutes 🕘

Focus

To help students produce the rhythm patterns of prepositional phrases.

Setup

Read the explanations and model the pronunciation of the examples. Have students listen to the audio and complete Exercise 1 individually before comparing answers with a partner. Then have the pairs take turns reading the sentences out loud. Circulate among pairs to monitor the use of rhythm patterns. Next, have students complete Exercise 2 individually before listening to the audio. Read the matched phrases, and have the students repeat them. Then have students work in pairs, taking turns reading the matched phrases to each other.

Expansion/Homework

You can do Exercise 2 as a dictation exercise. Have students close their books and write down what they hear. Read the matched phrases (e.g., *come to dinner/come tomorrow*). Then have students look at the phrases in the book to check their answers. Have them pronounce the matched phrases with a partner.

✪✪✪ B   STYLE: Using Descriptive Language

Suggested Time: 25 minutes 🕐

Focus

To get students to use descriptive language in preparation for storytelling.

Setup

Read the explanation and the examples in the box. If possible, you may want to bring in a rattle to demonstrate a rattling sound. Emphasize the importance of using descriptive language to make stories more interesting. Then have the students form groups of four (of different fluency levels, if possible) to complete Exercise 1. Make sure that students are seated in a circle. Have one group demonstrate the example. Then circulate among groups as they complete the activity to make sure they are including all three elements of descriptive language. Also, make sure they are writing down each sentence in its final form. Then have each group pick three favorite sentences to share with the class. Have students complete the listening task in Exercise 2.

Expansion/Homework

For additional practice, you may want to assign a few simple sentences using classmates' names. As homework, students can expand these sentences using the three elements of descriptive language. When they return to class, have them read their sentences to a partner. Then call on several students to share their sentences with the class.

✪✪ C   GRAMMAR: Infinitives of Purpose

Suggested Time: 20 minutes 🕐

Focus

To practice using infinitives of purpose to summarize events in a story.

Setup

Determine students' existing knowledge of the grammar point by having them read the dialogue and answer the questions in Exercise 1. Next, read the explanations and examples in the chart. Then have the students do Exercise 2 with a partner. Circulate among pairs to monitor their use of infinitives of purpose. When they are finished with this activity, read the instructions for Exercise 3, and have students work with the same partner. Remind students that an infinitive is used in response to a spoken question beginning with *why*. Also, remind them that *in order* is used with an infinitive in negative statements (as explained in the chart). Encourage them to make up an answer if they don't know it. Circulate among pairs and correct any grammatical errors that you hear. After the students have written down all the answers, have them compare answers with another pair. Then go over all the answers as a class.

Expansion/Homework

To save time, you can have students do Exercise 3 as homework and check it in class. For further practice, offer exercises from *Focus on Grammar, Intermediate*, and *Fundamentals of English Grammar*. See Grammar Book References on page 187 of the Student Book for specific units and chapters.

Link to *NorthStar: Reading and Writing*

You can ask students a few basic *Why?* questions about "The Metamorphosis" and have them respond by using infinitives of purpose.

 For extra listening practice, have students use the NorthStar Companion Video.

✪✪✪ D **SPEAKING TOPIC**

Suggested Time: 60 minutes 🕐

Focus

To give students a chance to develop their storytelling skills by creating a new ending to the "Lavender" story.

Setup

Read the instructions, and then place students in groups of three or four. (Place students who work well together in the same group.) Set a time limit for creating the stories. Next, set a time limit for practicing. Circulate among groups, making sure that students are following the instructions and creating a speaking part for each group member. Offer help as needed. Then have each group perform its story for the class.

Expansion/Homework

(1) If you have access to a video camera, you may want to videotape the performances so that students can view themselves later. (2) Encourage students to use props, costumes, and sound effects. (3) You may want to create award categories (i.e., Most Humorous Story, Most Frightening Story, Best Actor, Best Actress). Students can vote for the award winners after they have seen all the performances.

E RESEARCH TOPICS

LISTENING TO A STORY
Suggested Time: 30 minutes

Focus

To have students listen to a story and record their analysis and reaction.

Setup

Review the assignment with the students. Help them identify people who can tell them stories. It is not necessary for the stories to be told in English; the reporting task is more important. You may want to select a few of the best tapes to play for the whole class.

Expansion/Homework

In lieu of preparing a tape, the students can work in small groups (of classmates who work well together) to share information about the stories that they heard. They can use the same questions as a guideline for analysis and reaction.

DISCUSSING WELL-KNOWN STORIES
Suggested Time: 25 minutes

Focus

To give students the chance to interview others about well-known stories and to share their interview findings with classmates.

Setup

Have students meet in small groups (of classmates who work together well). Give them time to think of well-known stories or folktales. You may want to bring in a few picture books to help them think of examples. Help them identify people that they can interview about the stories. Go over the interview questions, and make sure the students are comfortable with them. After students have completed the interviews, have them work in groups to report on questions 3 and 4. You may want to conduct a class survey of all the stories that were selected and the different versions of each story that were discussed in the interviews.

Expansion/Homework
(1) The students can tape-record their interview results and give the tapes to you for review. (2) Students can choose well-known movies for their interview topics. (3) You may want to invite a storyteller to your class. Check your campus, local library, or community service club for possible storytellers. Your students might be able to recommend a fluent English speaker that they know, or perhaps they could translate a story being told in another language.

Separated by the Same Language

OVERVIEW	
Theme:	Language

Listenings:	Listening One: *Accent and Identity*
	    An interview
	Listening Two: *Code Switching*
	    A lecture on linguistics

Critical Thinking Skills:	Interpret a cartoon Recognize personal bias and stereotypes about accents Classify information Infer word meaning from context Interpret word usage Hypothesize scenarios Infer information not explicit in the listenings Hypothesize another's point of view Analyze problems and propose solutions
Listening Tasks:	Listen for main ideas Listen for details Listen closely to interpret a speaker's emotions Relate listening to personal values Take notes on a lecture Integrate information from two listenings Listen for specific information in student responses
Speaking Tasks:	Make predictions Pose and respond to questions Lead a group discussion Express and defend opinions Compare past and present abilities with modals Present a plan to improve English skills Present research on slang Conduct an interview and report findings
Pronunciation:	*Can/can't*
Vocabulary:	Word definitions Context clues
Grammar:	Modals of ability and possibility

UNIT SUMMARY

This unit explains various dialects and examines how dialect affects our sense of identity. Listening One is an interview between two graduate students about the experience one of them has had speaking a West Indies dialect in the United States. Listening Two is a lecture on code-switching and teenage slang.

The companion unit of *NorthStar: Reading and Writing* deals with how men and women use language differently.

1 Focus on the Topic, PAGE 73

✪✪✪A PREDICTING

Suggested Time: 10 minutes

Focus
To get students thinking about different ways of speaking the same language; to predict the content of the unit based on the cartoon and title.

Setup
Have students read questions 1–3. Read the cartoon out loud (simulating the accents, if you can). Discuss questions 1–3.

Expansion/Homework
You can ask students if, in their own language, they have experienced a situation similar to the one presented in the cartoon. You can also ask them if they know any other words associated with British English.

✪✪B SHARING INFORMATION

Suggested Time: 20 minutes

Focus
To encourage free discussion about accents in the students' native languages as a bridge to understanding the broader topic of dialects.

Setup
Have students respond to questions 1 and 2 individually. Then place them in small groups (of different language backgrounds, if possible) to discuss their answers. Go over their answers as a whole class. Try to focus on the features that "better" dialects seem to have in common (e.g., speakers' level of education).

Link to *NorthStar: Reading and Writing*
You can ask students to discuss how gender affects accent or speaking style. Some possible questions include: *Do men and women have different ways of speaking your native language? Are there certain words that only men or women use?*

✪✪✪ C **PREPARING TO LISTEN**

BACKGROUND
Suggested Time: 20 minutes 🕐

Focus
To present types of dialects in preparation for the listening; to familiarize students with the subject of linguistics.

Setup
Read the textbook excerpt and have students complete the matching exercise individually. Go over the answers as a class. Have the students work in small groups (of the same language background, if possible) to complete the discussion in Exercise 3. Elicit answers from each group, making sure to elicit at least one example of each type of dialect.

Expansion/Homework
This exercise can be done as homework, with class time spent checking answers and doing Exercise 3.

VOCABULARY FOR COMPREHENSION
Suggested Time: 15 minutes 🕐

Focus
To introduce vocabulary and concepts that students will encounter in Listening One to aid comprehension.

Setup
Have students complete the exercise individually before comparing answers with a partner. As a class, practice the pronunciation of the underlined words, and check the answers.

Expansion/Homework
To save time, you can assign this exercise as homework and use class time to work on pronunciation and to check answers.

2 Focus on Listening, PAGE 76

✪✪✪ A **LISTENING ONE: *Accent and Identity***
Suggested Time: 10 minutes 🕐

Focus
To encourage students to make a guess about the accent of Peter, one of the speakers; to become familiar with the speakers' voices.

Setup

Have the students look at the map before you play the excerpt. Encourage different predictions by calling on several students to answer each question. Affirm each prediction as a possibility.

✪✪✪ LISTENING FOR MAIN IDEAS
Suggested Time: 10 minutes 🕐

Focus
To help students understand the main ideas of the interview.

Setup
Play the interview through once without stopping. Have students choose the right answers while they listen. After listening, have student pairs exchange their books to compare answers before checking them as a class.

✪✪✪ LISTENING FOR DETAILS
Suggested Time: 15 minutes 🕐

Focus
To get students to listen for specific details in the interview.

Setup
Have students read the items and answer any they can. Play the interview and have students complete the statements. If students seem to be having trouble, play the interview one more time. Go over the answers. If disagreements arise, replay those segments rather than simply giving the answers.

✪✪ REACTING TO THE LISTENING
Suggested Time: 20 minutes 🕐

Focus
To encourage students to make inferences about Peter's feelings based on tone of voice and word choice.

Setup
Read the directions out loud. Play Excerpt 1 while students write their responses. Stop and discuss students' answers. Then play Excerpts 2–3, stopping between excerpts to give students time to write. Replay the excerpts if necessary. Then have students discuss their answers in class. If there is disagreement, use it as an opportunity for further discussion. Emphasize that students are welcome to have varying opinions, as long as their reasoning is sound. Put them in small groups (of similar fluency levels, if possible) to discuss the questions in Exercise 2. Call on individual students to share their answers with the class.

Expansion/Homework

You may want to add the following questions to the discussion: (a) *When you speak English, how often do people ask you where you are from? How do you feel about this question?* (b) *Do people ever make comments about your accent? What kind of comments do they make?* (c) *What do you think of different English dialects? Which ones sound clear? Which ones sound beautiful?*

✪✪✪ B | LISTENING TWO: *Code Switching*

Suggested Time: 10 minutes ⏱

Focus

To present information about teenage slang as an example of code switching; to familiarize students with academic note taking.

Setup

Have students look at the lecture notes. Read the introductory explanation. Then play the lecture, and have them complete the lecture notes. Go over the answers with the class, replaying any problematic segments.

✪✪✪ C | LINKING LISTENINGS ONE AND TWO

Suggested Time: 20 minutes ⏱

Focus

To allow students to integrate the information they heard in both listenings by comparing Peter's experience to that of an American teenager.

Setup

Read through the questions, making sure the students know how to respond to the chart in question 2. Next, have them work in pairs or small groups (of different language backgrounds, if possible). Call on various pairs or groups to share their answers with the class. Make sure that students give reasons for their answers to question 2. You may want to write their answers to question 3 on the board.

Link to *NorthStar: Reading and Writing*

You can use the following discussion questions: (a) *Are there times when men and women might want to change the way they speak? When?* (b) *Do you think men's and women's ways of speaking are an important part of their identities? Why or why not?* (c) *Do you think men and women use their ways of speaking as a way of fitting in? Explain.*

3 Focus on Vocabulary, PAGE 80

○ EXERCISE 1
Suggested Time: 15 minutes

Focus
To review new vocabulary from the unit.

Setup
Read the target words in the box, modeling their pronunciation. Then have students complete the exercise individually before checking answers with a partner. Go over the answers as a class.

Expansion/Homework
To provide additional pronunciation practice, you can have the students read the completed passage to each other in pairs, taking turns reading the sentences. Another option is to call on student volunteers to read each sentence of the completed passage.

○ EXERCISE 2
Suggested Time: 25 minutes

Focus
To give students the chance to use new vocabulary actively in real communication.

Setup
Explain the basic concept of Truth or Dare. This game might be unfamiliar to many students. Read through the instructions, making sure that students understand each step. Place the students in groups of five or six (of different language backgrounds, if possible). You might want to demonstrate the steps of the game using one group as a model. While the students play the game, circulate among the groups to monitor use of target vocabulary. Also, monitor the steps of the game. Make sure that students are choosing "truth" or "dare" options and responding to them appropriately. Be alert to any comments that might be hurtful or insulting to another classmate. Do everything you can to keep the game light and positive.

Link to *NorthStar: Reading and Writing*
You can have students select vocabulary from Unit 5 of the *Reading and Writing* book and use it to write more Truth or Dare questions. Choose the best questions, and play the game again. Use Unit 5 vocabulary for the "dares" in this game.

 For extra vocabulary practice, have students work on the self-grading vocabulary activities for the unit on the NorthStar Companion Website at **http://www.longman.com/northstar**.

4 Focus on Speaking, PAGE 82

✪✪ A   PRONUNCIATION: *Can/Can't*

Suggested Time: 15 minutes 🕒

Focus
To help students understand and pronounce *can* and *can't*.

Setup
Read the explanatory introduction, and play the examples. Next, read the chart, and pronounce the examples. Then have students complete Exercise 1 individually before checking their answers with a partner. Go over the answers as a class. Next, read the instructions for Exercise 2, and make sure the students know what to do. Have them complete Exercise 2 in the same pairs. Circulate among pairs to monitor their pronunciation of *can* and *can't*.

Expansion/Homework
You can provide more practice by having students take part in a chain drill. Place them in small groups (of different fluency levels) and have the first student begin by saying, *I can speak X, but I can't speak Y.* (Have them mention real languages that they can and cannot speak.) The next student repeats what the previous student has said and then adds his or her own sentence (e.g., *He can speak English, but he can't speak French. I can speak Spanish, but I can't speak Chinese.*). The chain drill continues until every student in the group has had a chance to speak.

✪✪✪ B   STYLE: Leading a Small Group Discussion

Suggested Time: 30 minutes 🕒

Focus
To give students a chance to lead and observe small group discussions.

Setup
Read through the instructions and phrases for leading a discussion. You may want to ask the students to add phrases to the list. Divide the class into groups of four (of similar fluency levels, if possible.) Read the instructions in Excercise 2 and circulate among groups as they complete the task. Make sure the groups are changing leaders every five minutes. You may want to give all students a chance to act as leader before having the observers share their notes with leaders.

Expansion/Homework
(1) You can have students write their own discussion questions using vocabulary and concepts from the unit. (2) You may want to select an exemplary group for videotaping. You can show the videotape to the class as an excellent example of small-group discussion.

Link to *NorthStar: Reading and Writing*
Students can add their own discussion questions using vocabulary and concepts from Unit 5.

✪✪ C   GRAMMAR: Modals of Ability and Possibility

Suggested Time: 25 minutes ⏱

Focus

To have students practice using modals to discuss their experiences and future plans in regard to improving their English.

Setup

Have the students read the paragraph and underline the modals. Then have them discuss questions 1–3 as a class. Next, read the explanatory chart. Have students work in pairs (of different language backgrounds, if possible) to do Exercise 2. Then have them write their answers to Exercise 3 individually, before sharing their answers with the same partner. Call on pairs to share their similarities with the class. Have them follow the example in the textbook.

Expansion/Homework

(1) You can have students evaluate their progress in English by ranking it on a scale of 1–5 (*1 = not satisfied at all with my progress; 5 = very satisfied with my progress*). Do a survey of the class to find out how students place themselves on the scale. Use the survey to identify the students who are very satisfied with their progress and the students who are not satisfied at all. The very satisfied students can then make suggestions to the others as follows: *You can do this . . . You could try doing that . . . You can also do this . . . You could do that.* Write their suggestions on the board and encourage discussion of the real challenges and opportunities that exist. (2) For further practice, offer exercises from *Focus on Grammar, Intermediate*, and *Fundamentals of English Grammar*. See Grammar Book References on page 187 of the Student Book for specific units and chapters.

 For extra listening practice, have students use the NorthStar Companion Video.

✪✪✪ D   SPEAKING TOPIC

Suggested Time: 50 minutes ⏱

Focus

To give students a chance to apply the vocabulary, concepts, and grammar they have learned in this unit.

Setup

Read the situations, and make sure that students understand each one. (You may need to explain that speakers in Mississippi have a regional accent that is sometimes stereotyped as uneducated.) Next, divide the class into groups of three or four students (who work well together). Make sure that they are prepared to use *could* and *should* in their discussion. You may need to explain that *could* describes future possibility, and *should* describes advice. Circulate among groups to make sure that their discussion is on track. Then give each group a chance to share their best solutions with the class. Encourage discussion by asking students to respond to each group. Possible questions include: (a) *Do you think he or she should do this? Why or why not?* (b) *What else could he or she do?*

Expansion/Homework

(1) These situations could be used as role-play activities. You can have students work in pairs (of similar fluency levels) to create role plays using the target vocabulary from the unit. If class time is limited, the role plays could be prepared outside of class and performed in class.

Link to *NorthStar: Reading and Writing*

Students can use the following situation as a basis for discussion and/or role play: *Monica is the only female manager in her company. She feels frustrated because the other managers, who are male, don't seem to take her seriously. Also, she doesn't like the way the other managers talk to each other because it seems rude. She is worried that she won't be able to fit in.* (If you choose to do this as a role play, have Monica discuss her problem with a friend who is a graduate student in linguistics.)

✪E   RESEARCH TOPICS

SLANG/JARGON RESEARCH
Suggested Time: 30–35 minutes 🕐

Focus
To give students a chance to learn more social dialects by researching slang and/or jargon.

Setup
Read the instructions, and help students identify people that they can interview. Make sure they understand that slang refers to informal, youth-oriented speech while jargon refers to technical speech within a professional field. Encourage them to use the Internet to add to their research. Then have them report back to the class individually by writing five slang or jargon words on the board and having their classmates guess their meaning before explaining them to the class.

Expansion/Homework
To save time, you can have the students report to small groups instead of the class. You can have each group select the most interesting words to share with the class.

ACCENT INTERVIEW
Suggested Time: 20 minutes 🕐

Focus
To give students a chance to learn more about dialects by interviewing someone with a different accent.

Setup

Read the instructions, and help students identify people that they can interview. The person can be either a native or non-native speaker of English. The interview can be done inside or outside of class. To facilitate the group work, give the students a list of Peter's key points concerning accent and identity. You may wish to create this list with the students as a review. Place students in groups that work well together. You may want to have each group share the results of the most interesting interview with the whole class.

Expansion/Homework

You can invite a guest speaker to visit the class and share his or her experiences with accent and identity. You can select someone with a different regional or social accent, or you may want to select an advanced non-native speaker of English. Have your students prepare questions for the speaker using key vocabulary from the unit.

UNIT 6

Culture and Commerce

Theme:	Tourism

Listenings:	Listening One: *Radio News Report*
	   A report on the Pa Daung tribe
	Listening Two: *Town Hall Meeting in Hyannis, Cape Cod*
	   Two opposing views on tourism

Critical Thinking Skills:	Recognize personal assumptions about tourism Evaluate the advantages and disadvantages of tourism Infer word meaning from context Support opinions with reasons Hypothesize outcomes Compare and contrast vacation experiences
Listening Tasks:	Listen for main ideas Listen for details Interpret speaker's tone and emotions Identify contrasting viewpoints in the listening Synthesize information from two listenings Categorize end sounds Take a dictation Listen to student presentations and pose questions
Speaking Tasks:	Make predictions Express and defend opinions Use new vocabulary in an open conversation Tell a story using transition words Interview a classmate Summarize an interview Outline, rehearse, and present a three-minute speech Present a poster session about a local tourist attraction
Pronunciation:	Past tense endings
Vocabulary:	Context clues Word definitions Vocabulary classification
Grammar:	Simple past tense

UNIT SUMMARY

This unit explores the positive and negative aspects of tourism. Listening One is a news report on travel to the Pa Daung region of Thailand, which is known for its long-necked women. Listening Two is a town hall meeting in which participants discuss tourism in Cape Cod.

The companion unit of *NorthStar: Reading and Writing* deals with positive and negative aspects of ecotourism, which involves travel to endangered natural environments such as Antarctica.

1 Focus on the Topic, PAGE 91

✪✪✪ A   PREDICTING

Suggested Time: 5 minutes ⏱

Focus
To introduce the topic of long-necked women of the Pa Daung tribe; to predict the unit content.

Setup
Have students look at the title and the picture, hypothesize about the unit's content, and discuss questions 1 and 2 as a class. You may need to define *commerce* for the students.

Note: Be prepared for strong reactions to this topic from some students, who may express feelings ranging from fascination to disgust. Encourage a variety of answers to the questions.

✪✪ B   SHARING INFORMATION

Suggested Time: 20 minutes 🖉

Focus
To encourage free discussion of the students' attitudes toward tourism and commercialization.

Setup
Read through the statements, and define any unfamiliar vocabulary. Elicit examples of local tourist attractions to clarify understanding. Make sure the students understand how to indicate their degree of agreement or disagreement. After they respond to the statements individually, place them in small groups (of different fluency levels, if possible) to compare their responses. Call on each group to share their opinions with the class. Encourage students to give reasons for their opinions.

Expansion/Homework

You can call on volunteers to read each statement out loud while students mark their individual responses.

✪✪✪ C   PREPARING TO LISTEN

BACKGROUND
Suggested Time: 15 minutes 🕐

Focus

To provide more information about the topic of tourism in the Pa Daung region; to have students consider the positive and negative aspects of this type of tourism.

Setup

Call on students to read each section of the brochure. Then have them discuss the questions in small groups (of different fluency levels, if possible). Call on each group to share their answers to question 3. List their ideas on the board. If possible, ask them to consider the positive and negative aspects of tourism in their own local area.

Expansion/Homework

You may want to conduct a class survey. Ask the students in each small group to give you their answers to question 1. Keep a tally on the board of how many students are interested in taking the Pa Daung tour.

Link to *NorthStar: Reading and Writing*

You can ask students to compare traveling to the Pa Daung region to traveling to Antarctica. Possible questions might include: (a) *Which tour seems more interesting to you? Why?* (b) *How much would you spend on each tour?*

VOCABULARY FOR COMPREHENSION
Suggested Time: 15 minutes 🕐

Focus

To introduce vocabulary related to tourism to aid students in comprehension of the listening.

Setup

Practice pronunciation of the underlined words with the class. Then have students read the e-mails and select the definitions individually before comparing their answers with a partner's. Go over the answers as a class.

Expansion/Homework

To save time, you can assign the exercise as homework and use class time to work on pronunciation and check answers.

② Focus on Listening, PAGE 95

❄❄❄ A ▐ **LISTENING ONE:** *Radio News Report*

Suggested Time: 5 minutes ⏱

Focus

To encourage students to predict the tone of the news report; to help students become familiar with the speaker's voice.

Setup

Read the instructions for the prediction activity. Play the excerpt from the news report, and have students mark their choices as they listen. Call on several students to share their predictions with the class. Affirm each prediction as a possibility.

✪✪✪ **LISTENING FOR MAIN IDEAS**

Suggested Time: 15 minutes ⏱

Focus

To help students understand the main topics in the news report.

Setup

Have students read the directions and the multiple-choice statements. Play the news report once, and have students circle the best answer for each question. Ask students to compare answers with a partner before checking them as a class.

✪✪✪ **LISTENING FOR DETAILS**

Suggested Time: 15 minutes ⏱

Focus

To help students listen for specific details in the news report.

Setup

Ask students to read the items and answer the ones they know. Play the news report, and have students label the statements true or false. Have students compare answers with those of a partner. If disagreements arise, replay those segments rather than simply giving the answers.

Expansion/Homework

Check the answers by having volunteers write one answer each on the board. Compare answers in class.

✪✪ **REACTING TO THE LISTENING**

Suggested Time: 20 minutes ⏱

Focus

To help students make inferences about Pa Daung women's feelings based on tone of voice; to help students understand the arguments that tourists use while discussing their opinions about tourism in the Pa Daung region.

Setup

Read the directions in Exercise 1 out loud. Go over the adjectives, and make sure that students understand each one. Play Excerpt 1 while students fill out the chart. Stop and discuss students' answers. Then play Excerpt 2 while students fill out the chart. Replay the excerpts if necessary. As you discuss answers, emphasize that students are welcome to express varying opinions, as long as their reasoning is sound. Next, read the directions in Exercise 2 out loud. Play the tourists' comments while the students take notes. Repeat the audio if necessary. Then call on individual students to share their answers to questions 2 and 3.

Expansion/Homework

(1) For Exercise 1, you may want to play the excerpts again and ask students to think about what the women are saying. After replaying Excerpt 1, ask them to consider other forms of body art that cannot be reversed. Some examples include piercing, tattoos, and foot-binding. Ask them to compare the long-necked women to entertainers and models who undergo surgery and weight loss to make a living. After replaying Excerpt 2, ask them to evaluate the women's lives now compared to their lives in Myanmar (formerly Burma). Ask the students which life they would prefer: performing menial labor or posing for tourist cameras. (2) For Exercise 2, you may want to have the students prepare their answers to questions 2 and 3 as homework. When they return to class, you can place them in groups according to which side they agree with. Give them a few minutes to compare their arguments. Then appoint a group spokesperson to present their arguments to the class.

✪✪✪ B LISTENING TWO: *Town Hall Meeting in Hyannis, Cape Cod*

Suggested Time: 10 minutes ⏱

Focus

To broaden students' understanding of the positive and negative aspects of tourism; to give students experience with a different kind of listening.

Setup

Ask students if they know what a town hall meeting is. Discuss briefly why someone might attend a town hall meeting. Look at the map and related information. Ask the students to discuss possible reasons why Cape Cod is attractive to tourists. Then read the second set of directions, and have students answer the questions as you play the town hall meetings. Go over the answers, replaying any problematic segments.

✪✪✪ C LINKING LISTENINGS ONE AND TWO

Suggested Time: 15 minutes ⏱

Focus

To get students to integrate information from both listenings by reviewing the positive and negative aspects of tourism that have been presented.

Setup

For question 1, read the directions and the accompanying chart. Next, read question 2. Then give students time to jot down a few similarities in the chart and think about question 2 individually. After this, have them work in groups (of different language backgrounds, if possible) to share their ideas. Call on each group to share its answers with the whole class. List the positive and negative aspects of tourism on the board.

Expansion/Homework

Students can dramatize the effects of a decrease in tourism through role play. Divide the class into pairs and have them select the roles of Pa Daung tribespeople or Cape Cod residents. Give them the following scenario: *Tourism in your area has decreased. Discuss how this decrease has affected your lives. Include at least one positive and one negative effect in your discussion. State whether or not you are happy with this decrease.* Give the students time to prepare their role play and call on several volunteer pairs to perform for the class.

Link to *NorthStar: Reading and Writing*

You can ask students to discuss the positive and negative aspects of ecotourism as well as the effects of a decrease in tourism on fragile environments such as Antarctica.

❸ Focus on Vocabulary, PAGE 100

✪ EXERCISES 1 AND 2
Suggested Time: 15 minutes 🕙

Focus

To review vocabulary from the unit by focusing on the positive, negative, and neutral meaning of words.

Setup

Read the instructions, and go over the examples of positive, negative, and neutral meaning of words. Elicit a few more examples of each type. Next, have students work in pairs (of different language backgrounds, if possible) to complete the chart in Exercise 1. Then have students meet with neighboring pairs to discuss Exercise 2 before going over their answers as a class. Encourage discussion, and if disagreement arises, allow students to give reasons for their choices.

Expansion/Homework

You can have students do Exercises 1 and 2 for homework. When they return to class, have them compare their answers with those of several different classmates. Tell students to move freely around the room with their books, checking their answers with those of three other students. Ask them to mark any answers that were different from their classmates', and discuss these as a class.

✪ EXERCISE 3
Suggested Time: 20 minutes

Focus
To give students a chance to use new vocabulary actively in real communication.

Setup
Review the pronunciation of the underlined words. Then have volunteer students read each question out loud before dividing the class into small groups (of different fluency levels, if possible). Circulate among groups to monitor their use of new vocabulary. Listen to their discussion, and then call on a few groups to share interesting ideas with the class.

Expansion/Homework
(1) You can assign these questions to individual students to prepare outside of class. Then students can give brief oral presentations in response to their assigned question. (2) These questions can be assigned as audio journal topics. Depending on the size of your class, you may want to have students choose a limited number of questions for use as audio journal topics.

Link to *NorthStar: Reading and Writing*
You can list vocabulary items from Unit 6 on the board, and encourage students to use them in their discussion.

 For extra vocabulary practice, have students work on the self-grading vocabulary activities for the unit on the NorthStar Companion Website at **http://www.longman.com/northstar**.

4 Focus on Speaking, PAGE 101

✪✪ A PRONUNCIATION: Past Tense Endings
Suggested Time: 20 minutes

Focus
To give students a chance to practice the three past tense endings that go with regular past tense verbs.

Setup
Read the rules and examples in the chart. Model the pronunciation of the three word endings. Review voiced and voiceless consonants as needed. Next, read the instructions for Exercise 1, and play the audio. Then have students complete Exercise 2 by checking their answers with a partner, and taking turns reading each verb out loud. Go over the pronunciation of each verb tense ending as a whole class. Next, read the instructions for Exercise 3. Have students work with the same partner to read the sentences that they have completed.

Expansion/Homework

To check your students' grammatical usage, you can have students write ten sentences as homework. In each sentence, have them describe something that they did on a recent vacation (real or imagined). When they return to class, have them read their sentences aloud to a partner. Circulate among pairs, and monitor their pronunciation of past tense verb endings. Have students write sentences on the board representing each of the three past tense endings. Pronounce the sentences as a class.

✪✪✪ B | STYLE: Transitions for Storytelling

Suggested Time: 25 minutes ⏱

Focus

To give students practice using transitions in storytelling.

Setup

Read the introduction and example story. Go over the transition words in the chart, making it clear that transitions are used at the beginning, middle, and end of stories. Next, read the instructions for the activity. Have students form groups of three or four (of similar fluency levels, if possible) and sit in circles facing each other. Go over the example, and make sure students understand that they must add details to the story. Encourage them to use humorous details. Circulate among groups to monitor their use of transitions. Make sure that students approach this as a speaking activity. Some students may be inclined to write their sentences down; encourage them to practice speaking naturally and fluently.

Expansion/Homework

(1) You can choose two or three well-developed stories to be shared with the whole class. One option is to have the group of storytellers come to the front of the class and tell their story. Encourage them to tell the story dramatically, and allow them to refer to notes if necessary. Another option is to have students dictate their stories to you. Underline transitions as you write them on the board. The stories can then be read aloud by the whole class. (2) You can provide more storytelling practice by giving students a picture of a travel destination such as Tahiti, Alaska, or Paris, and having them create a story about an imaginary trip to this place. Then have them tell their stories to the class, using appropriate transitions.

Link to *NorthStar: Reading and Writing*

You can have students create an additional story as homework or an audio journal topic. Have them tell the story of visiting Antarctica, using transitions at the beginning, middle, and end of the story.

✪✪ C | GRAMMAR: Simple Past Tense

Suggested Time: 30 minutes ⏱

Focus

To help students use regular and irregular past tense verbs in real communication.

Setup

Have students read the e-mail in Exercise 1 and circle the past tense verbs. Next, have them discuss question 2 before reading the explanatory chart. Then have students complete Exercise 2 in pairs (of different language backgrounds, if possible). Circulate among pairs, and monitor their use of regular and irregular past tense verbs. Then have each student share information about his or her partner as directed in Exercise 3. Make sure that students understand the listening task implied in Exercise 3. Encourage them to take notes while each classmate shares information so that they can give examples to explain their answers. If there is disagreement, allow a variety of answers as long as students can support their ideas with examples.

Expansion/Homework

(1) Depending on the size of your class, you may not have time to allow every classmate to share information about his or her partner. You may want to have half the students share during one class session, and half the students share during another. (2) The questions in Exercise 2 can also be used for an interview. Have students interview two or three people (preferably native speakers) outside of class and record the interview results in their audio journals. They can use the questions in Exercise 3 to evaluate the information they obtain. (3) For further practice, offer exercises from *Focus on Grammar, Intermediate*, and *Fundamentals of English Grammar*. See the Grammar Book References on page 187 of the Student Book for specific units and chapters.

 For extra listening practice, have students use the NorthStar Companion Video.

✪✪✪ D   SPEAKING TOPIC

Suggested Time: 50 minutes 🕐

Focus

To give students a chance to use the knowledge, vocabulary, and skills they have acquired from the unit to give an oral presentation on a tourist experience.

Setup

Read the directions, and review the meaning of the suggested adjectives. Have the students prepare their presentations individually. Make sure that they include both a summarizing and concluding sentence. Remind them to stay within the two-minute time limit. As each student speaks to the class, have the listeners write down a question. If class time is limited, you may want to collect the questions instead of discussing them. The purpose of the questions is to make sure that each classmate is listening attentively. You may want to select the most interesting questions for a follow-up discussion.

Expansion/Homework

If you want the presentations to be more polished, you can give students more preparation time and have them prepare visuals (e.g., pictures, charts, PowerPoint presentations) to accompany their talks. You may also want to require that they use notecards and/or memorize their speeches.

✪ E   RESEARCH TOPICS

POSTER PRESENTATION
Suggested Time: 30 minutes ⊕

Focus
To have students gather more information about tourist destinations; to give students practice explaining information to an audience.

Setup
If possible, bring in travel posters and brochures to use as examples. These are commonly available at travel agencies. Read the directions, and help students identify tourist information centers and travel agencies in their local area. Encourage them to use the Internet as well. After the students have prepared their posters, follow the directions for displaying the posters in class and presenting the information. Be sure to switch roles so that everyone has a chance to present information to the class.

Expansion/Homework
(1) If you have access to PowerPoint technology, the students can prepare PowerPoint presentations instead of posters. Keep in mind that this approach will require more class time for the presentations. (2) You can create award categories such as Most Artistic, Most Informative, Most Unusual and have the class vote on award-winning posters. These can be displayed on the class bulletin board.

Link to *NorthStar: Reading and Writing*
Encourage students to create posters depicting ecotourism locations such as Antarctica, the Amazon, Costa Rica, and Thailand.

SURVEY
Suggested Time: 25 minutes ⊕

Focus
To gather information on a local tourist attraction; to give students practice conversing with native speakers and summarizing survey results.

Setup
Read the directions and help the students identify local tourist attractions in their area. Next, help them identify people whom they can interview. Go over the survey questions, and practice asking interview subjects for their help in completing the survey. Coach the students on using the survey questions as guidelines for preparing a short presentation. One suggested format is as follows: *This place is so popular with tourists because. . . . Some of the positive effects of tourism in this area. . . .* etc. Encourage the students to give clear, concise presentations.

Expansion/Homework

(1) If the number of tourist attractions is limited, you might have students work in small groups to conduct a survey on an assigned tourist attraction. If possible, assign a different attraction to each group to avoid repetition. Have each group member conduct the survey individually, and then give the group members time to pool their information. Appoint a spokesperson from each group to present the survey findings to the class. (2) If native speakers of English are not available, the surveys can be conducted in the local language. (3) Some students may not have tape recorders; in this case, allow them to take notes while they conduct the survey. (4) If your local area has a tourist information center, you might be able to invite a spokesperson to come and speak to the class on local attractions, and the positive and negative effects of tourism in your area. Students can record their responses to the guest speaker as an audio journal assignment.

Joking Around

OVERVIEW

Theme:	Humor
Listenings:	Listening One: *What's So Funny?* 　　An interview with a sociologist Listening Two: *More Jokes* 　　Eight jokes
Critical Thinking Skills:	Interpret jokes Compare personal preferences in humor Infer word meaning from context Classify types of jokes Distinguish between ironic and non-ironic statements Draw conclusions Evaluate and rank quality of jokes
Listening Tasks:	Identify main ideas Listen for details Interpret speaker's tone of voice Compare observations in listening to one's personal 　　observations Listen to jokes and predict punch lines Decipher words spoken with reduced pronunciation Take notes on student information
Speaking Tasks:	Make predictions Give examples to illustrate new vocabulary Compose and tell original jokes Discuss preferences in entertainment Ask for repetition or clarification Ask and answer questions in an information gap activity Practice telling and reacting to jokes
Pronunciation:	Reduction of *h* in pronouns
Vocabulary:	Word definitions Phrasal verbs Context clues
Grammar:	*Wh-* questions

UNIT SUMMARY

This unit explores the topic of humor by presenting different types of jokes. Listening One is a call-in radio program featuring a sociologist who studies humor. Callers respond to his presentation by calling in with jokes. Listening Two presents more jokes.

   The companion unit of *NorthStar: Reading and Writing* presents the autobiography of Lucille Ball and includes a critical review of "The Cosby Show."

1 Focus on the Topic, PAGE 109

✪✪✪ A PREDICTING

Suggested Time: 5 minutes ⏱

Focus

To get students thinking about the general topic of jokes; to have them use the title of the unit to predict the content.

Setup

Have students look at the cartoon and discuss the questions. Then have students look at the title and discuss what they think the unit will be about.

Expansion/Homework

You may want to have students jot down answers to the questions and compare their answers with those of the student sitting next to them before the class discussion.

✪✪ B SHARING INFORMATION

Suggested Time: 20 minutes ⏱

Focus

To encourage free discussion about the types of humor that students enjoy and that are popular in their home cultures.

Setup

Divide students into small groups (of different language backgrounds, if possible). Next, have them answer the questions individually before sharing their answers in the group. Then call on various groups to share their answers with the class.

Expansion/Homework

You can tally the answers to question 1 on the board to create a class survey. Encourage cross-cultural comparisons, if possible.

✪✪✪ C ▎**PREPARING TO LISTEN**

BACKGROUND
Suggested Time: 15 minutes ⏱

Focus
To introduce students to various types of jokes.

Setup
Read the explanation of each joke type, and have volunteer students read the jokes out loud. Discuss each joke, and make sure that students understand its meaning. Ask a few individual students to choose the two jokes they like best and explain why they like them. Elicit more examples of each type of joke, if possible.

Expansion/Homework
One way to elicit more examples is to have students work in pairs (of the same language background, if possible). First, ask them to think of other jokes in English that correspond to each type. Next, have them think of similar jokes in their native languages. If possible, have them translate these jokes into English. Then call on each pair to share jokes with the class.

VOCABULARY FOR COMPREHENSION
Suggested Time: 15 minutes ⏱

Focus
To introduce vocabulary and concepts about humor in preparation for the listening.

Setup
Ask students to pronounce the underlined words. Then pair students up to read the dialogues, and choose the definitions. Then go over the answers as a class.

Expansion/Homework
To save time, you can assign the exercise as homework and use class time to work on pronunciation and check answers.

2 Focus on Listening, PAGE 114

✪✪✪ A ▎**LISTENING ONE: *What's So Funny?***
Suggested Time: 10 minutes ⏱

Focus
To encourage students to make predictions about the content of the radio program; to help them become familiar with the speakers' voices.

Setup

Before listening to the excerpt, let students know that the audio is based on a real radio show, and have them answer question 1. Then play the excerpt, and have them predict the answers to questions 2 and 3. Ask students to share their predictions with a partner. Affirm each prediction as a possibility.

✪✪✪ LISTENING FOR MAIN IDEAS
Suggested Time: 10 minutes ⏱

Focus

To help students identify the main points of the radio program.

Setup

Allow students to read the questions and multiple choice answers. Then play the listening once. Have students select the answers while they listen. After listening, have students compare their answers in pairs before checking them as a class.

✪✪✪ LISTENING FOR DETAILS
Suggested Time: 15 minutes ⏱

Focus

To help students refine their understanding of the listening.

Setup

Have students read the statements and answer the items that they already know. Then play the listening again all the way through while students complete the statements. If students seem to be having trouble, play the listening one more time. Go over the answers. If disagreements arise, replay those segments rather than simply giving answers.

✪✪ REACTING TO THE LISTENING
Suggested Time: 25 minutes 🎙

Focus

To help students understand irony as a form of humor; to listen for irony in a speaker's tone of voice; to evaluate important ideas from the listening.

Setup

Read the explanation, and make sure that students understand the concept of irony. Play the excerpts from the listening. Stop after each excerpt, if necessary, to allow students time to fill in the chart. After students have discussed the answers with a partner, discuss them as a class. Allow disagreement as long as students' reasoning is sound. Then have them work in small groups (of different fluency levels, if possible) to discuss the statements in Exercise 2. Call on each group to share their answers with the class.

Expansion/Homework

Encourage students to think of examples to support the statements in Exercise 2. For example, have them think of a social situation in which people might use humor in order to bond with each other (e.g., making a toast at a wedding reception; telling a joke at the beginning of a speech).

Link to *NorthStar: Reading and Writing*

You can have students discuss slapstick humor (as exemplified by Lucille Ball) and consider whether this form of humor is ever used for the reasons described in Exercise 2.

✪✪✪ B LISTENING TWO: *More Jokes*

Suggested Time: 20 minutes 🕐

Focus

To present other jokes; to listen specifically for punch lines.

Setup

Tell students that they will hear more jokes. Have students read the punch lines before you play the listening. Have students match the jokes with punch lines as they listen. Then go over the answers, replaying any jokes that they don't understand. Have students explain the meaning of each joke.

✪✪✪ C LINKING LISTENINGS ONE AND TWO

Suggested Time: 15 minutes 🕐

Focus

To get students to classify jokes from Listening Two according to the information presented in Listening One.

Setup

Read the instructions for Exercise 1. Give students time to read the lists of punch lines and joke types. Then play the listening while students match the punch line to the type of joke. Next, have students compare their answers with a partner's before going over the answers as a whole class. Then read the instructions for Exercise 2, and have the students discuss it with their partners before discussing it with the class.

Link to *NorthStar: Reading and Writing*

(1) You can ask students to consider which type of joke is most suitable for television comedy. (2) You can also have students watch a current television comedy and report on the types of jokes that are included. Students can present the reports to their classmates or record them in their audio journals.

❸ Focus on Vocabulary, PAGE 118

✪ EXERCISE 1
Suggested Time: 25 minutes 🕐

Focus
To review vocabulary from the unit in the context of a crossword puzzle.

Setup
Review the instructions, and make sure the students know how to do a crossword puzzle. Have the students work in pairs (of different language backgrounds, if possible) to complete the puzzle. Review the answers as a class. If you have access to an overhead projector, make a transparency of the puzzle with completed answers to save time during review.

Expansion/Homework
You can turn this activity into a game by having students work in small teams to complete the crossword puzzle within a time limit.

Link to *NorthStar: Reading and Writing*
You can challenge students to work in pairs to create a crossword puzzle using new vocabulary from Unit 7. First, have them write definitions and create a crossword grid. Then have them give copies of the puzzle to their classmates to solve.

✪ EXERCISE 2
Suggested Time: 20 minutes 🕐

Focus
To build on the vocabulary of the unit by having students use new words in real communication.

Setup
Read the instructions, and then divide the class into small groups (of different fluency levels, if possible). Circulate among groups to make sure that students are using target vocabulary and giving themselves points for each example. Set a time limit and have each group tell you the name of the student with the highest number of points. Reward the student with the highest number of points (with applause, candy, or other small prize). If time allows, elicit answers to each question.

Expansion/Homework
Some of these items are more difficult than others, so you may want to award 2–3 points for these.

For extra vocabulary practice, have students work on the self-grading vocabulary activities for the unit on the NorthStar Companion Website at **http://www.longman.com/northstar**.

4 Focus on Speaking, PAGE 120

✪✪A PRONUNCIATION: Reduction of *h* in Pronouns

Suggested Time: 25 minutes 🕙

Focus
To have students practice the reduction of *h* in unstressed pronouns.

Setup
Read the explanation and examples. Then play the listening examples for students to repeat. Next, read the instructions for Exercise 2, and have students complete it individually before having them check answers with a partner. Then have students take turns reading the jokes to each other. Monitor their pronunciation of unstressed pronouns. Next, do one example of Exercise 4 as a class. Give students time to write three jokes individually before walking around the room to share them with classmates. Listen as students share their jokes and choose two or three clever ones to be told to the whole class.

Expansion/Homework
Students can do Exercise 4 as an audio journal assignment. After they record their jokes, choose five or six to play for the class. Have students write down the punch lines. To add some fun, you can have them try to guess which classmate's voice is being played.

✪✪✪B STYLE: Asking for Repetition or Clarification

Suggested Time: 25 minutes 🕙

Focus
To help students improve their listening comprehension by learning how to ask for repetition or clarification.

Setup
With books closed, ask students what they say if they can't understand someone. Put some of their answers on the board. Then, with open books, ask students to look at the chart. Explain any expressions that were not in the students' list. Next, have students complete Exercise 1 individually. Then have them work in pairs (of different fluency levels, if possible) to complete Exercise 2. Circulate among pairs to monitor their use of the new expressions. After students change roles, have them exchange books to make sure that they have written the correct information.

Expansion/Homework
For additional practice, you can create a role play. First, have each pair choose a joke from the unit. Then Student A begins by saying, *Do you want to hear a good joke?* Then he or she tells the joke as quickly as possible. Student B asks for clarification and repetition before finishing the role play with, *OK. Now I get it!* After giving students adequate time to practice, call on several pairs to perform their role play for the class.

Link to *NorthStar: Reading and Writing*

You can have students prepare a brief report on a television or film comedy to present to a small group of classmates. As they present their reports, have other students ask for clarification or repetition. After the reports have been given, have each group share its most interesting report with the whole class.

✪✪ C   GRAMMAR: *Wh-* Questions

Suggested Time: 25 minutes

Focus

To give students practice using *wh-* questions in real communication.

Setup

Look at the photo of Jerry Seinfeld and discuss the questions in Exercise 1 before looking at Exercise 2. Elicit answers to the questions in Exercise 2, and then read the explanation. Before starting the information gap activity in Exercise 3, make sure that students understand how to form *wh-* questions by giving them a few statements and having them change the statements into questions, for example: (a) *Jerry Seinfeld is married./Who is married?* (b) *Jerry Seinfeld has a daughter./What does he have?* Then explain the information gap activity, and have students work in pairs (of different fluency levels, if possible). Circulate among pairs to monitor their use of *wh-* questions. Help students as needed as they write their questions, and listen as they ask each other questions. Then go over the answers as a class.

Expansion/Homework

(1) Bring in photos of comedians that the students know (e.g., Jim Carrey, Adam Sandler). You can also have the students bring in photos of other celebrities such as singers and movie stars. Divide the class into two or more teams, and award points to each team member who can ask a grammatically correct *wh-* question about one of the photos. Award a point to members of other teams who can answer the question correctly. (2) For further practice, offer exercises from *Focus on Grammar, Intermediate*, and *Fundamentals of English Grammar*. See Grammar Book References on page 187 of the Student Book for specific units and chapters.

Link to *NorthStar: Reading and Writing*

For expansion activity 1 above you can bring in photos of Lucille Ball and Bill Cosby.

 For extra listening practice, have students use the NorthStar Companion Video.

✪✪✪ D SPEAKING TOPIC

Suggested Time: 30 minutes 🕘

Focus
To give students a chance to use the knowledge, vocabulary, and skills they have acquired from the unit; to practice telling and listening to jokes; to evaluate a variety of jokes.

Setup
Read the instructions, and divide the class into ten groups. Make sure that students understand the three options they have in responding to the jokes they hear. Be available to support and guide students as they move around the class. Since some students may finish this activity more quickly than others, you may want to have the students who finish early meet together to discuss the meaning of each joke. Then complete Step 5 as a class.

Expansion/Homework
You can assign each of the ten jokes to individual students to record for the class to listen to in small groups. The groups can rank the jokes, and ask for clarification of ones they don't understand. Then as a class you can explain the meaning of each joke and vote on the funniest.

✪ E RESEARCH TOPICS

JOKE SEARCH AND JOKE TRANSLATION
Suggested Time: 20 minutes 🕘

Focus
To have students discover and share new jokes; to give students a chance to share a joke from their native cultures.

Setup
Read the assignments. For both options, have students tell their jokes individually to the class. For option 2, have students post their jokes on the wall so that others can learn it.

Expansion/Homework
(1) You can create a class bulletin board to post jokes from both options. You can also have a student with access to desktop publishing prepare a "joke page" listing jokes that have been shared with the class. Distribute the joke page among classmates for their future joke-telling pleasure. (2) If your school is located near a comedy club, you might want to take the students to see a professional comedian. Have them keep track of the different types of jokes that they hear. Also, have them discuss the meaning of a joke that they understood and enjoyed. Before you attend the club, be sure to preview the comic's material to make sure that it is appropriate for your class.

Traditional or Trendy?

OVERVIEW	
Theme:	Fashion

Listenings:	Listening One: *Interview with Shanika De Silva*
	        A conversation about Sri Lankan fashion
	Listening Two: *Interview with a Fashion Designer*
	        A conversation about current fashion trends

Critical Thinking Skills:	Compare and contrast two types of dress Compare cultural norms of dress Interpret word usage Analyze the advantages and disadvantages of traditional dress Hypothesize point of view Compare and contrast points of view Analyze relationships between words Interpret the significance of how a person dresses
Listening Tasks:	Identify main topics Listen for details Interpret speaker's attitude Relate listening to personal values Identify a speaker's point of view Synthesize information from two listenings Identify thought groups in speech Listen to student presentations and answer questions
Speaking Tasks:	Make predictions Express opinions Give impromptu definitions of new vocabulary Group words for appropriate intonation and meaning Manipulate intonation to change meaning of a sentence Describe changes in fashion using the phrase *used to* Outline, rehearse, and present an introduction to an oral report Give an impromptu presentation using an outline to quickly organize ideas and notes Give an oral report on research
Pronunciation:	Thought groups
Vocabulary:	Context clues Definitions Synonyms Analogies
Grammar:	*Used to*

UNIT SUMMARY

This unit examines the feelings people have about traditional clothing as their cultures change due to travel, immigration, colonization, and other influences. Listening One is an interview with a Sri Lankan woman, who lives in the United States, about traditional clothing in her country and her changing feelings about traditional dress. Listening Two is an interview with a fashion designer about clothing at work.

The companion unit in *NorthStar: Reading and Writing* deals with the growing popularity of cosmetic surgery.

1 Focus on the Topic, PAGE 127

✪✪✪A PREDICTING

Suggested Time: 5 minutes ⏱

Focus
To get students thinking about the factors that influence how we dress; to examine the meaning of the title and use it to predict the unit content.

Setup
Have students look at the photos and discuss question 1. Show where Sri Lanka is on a map and have students discuss questions 2 and 3 in small groups (of different language backgrounds, if possible). Then elicit students' thoughts on question 3, and write them on the board.

Expansion/Homework
You may want to ask students to consider if they are "traditional" or "trendy." Ask them to explain their ideas.

✪✪B SHARING INFORMATION

Suggested Time: 20 minutes ⏱

Focus
To encourage free discussion of students' fashion and clothing choices; to explore the topic of traditional clothing in the students' home countries.

Setup
Divide students into groups of three (from different cultures, if possible), and have them discuss questions 1 and 2. While students are talking, make a chart on the board that lists all the nationalities in the class on the left, followed by one column labeled *Traditional Clothing* and one labeled *When People Wear It*. Reconvene and ask selected students to write information in the two columns. Discuss the chart and get students to make generalizations (e.g., *Which culture seems to have the most traditional clothing?*).

Expansion/Homework

(1) You may want to have students bring in pictures of people (preferably themselves) wearing traditional clothing from their culture. Give this assignment the night before so that they can show the pictures when discussing question 2. (2) If all your students are from the same culture, you can ask them to discuss how clothing choices in the United States, and other countries, differ from those in their home cultures.

Link to *NorthStar: Reading and Writing*

You can add the following discussion questions: *In your culture, do people spend a lot of time on hair and makeup? What kind of jewelry or body art do people wear? Is cosmetic surgery common?*

✪✪✪ C   PREPARING TO LISTEN

BACKGROUND
Suggested Time: 15 minutes ⏱

Focus
To introduce students to the culture of Sri Lanka; to compare the traditional clothing of Sri Lanka to that of other cultures; to consider the advantages and disadvantages of traditional clothing.

Setup
Look at the map and read the first paragraph about Sri Lanka. Next, look at the illustration of traditional clothing, and ask a student volunteer to read the second paragraph. Then discuss the questions as a class.

Expansion/Homework
You may want to use question 2 as an exercise to practice expressing opinions. Before dividing students into groups, practice language for stating opinions and giving reasons (e.g., *I think one advantage is . . . because . . .*). Then have students work in small groups (of different language backgrounds, if possible) to discuss question 2. Circulate among groups to monitor their skills in expressing opinions.

VOCABULARY FOR COMPREHENSION
Suggested Time: 15 minutes ⏱

Focus
To introduce vocabulary related to Sri Lankan traditional dress to aid in comprehension of the listening.

Setup
Have students pronounce the underlined words, and then have them do the matching in pairs (of different fluency levels, if possible). Go over the answers as a class.

Expansion/Homework
To save time, you can assign the matching as homework and use class time to work on pronunciation and to check answers.

② Focus on Listening, PAGE 130

✪✪✪ A ⬛ LISTENING ONE: *Interview with Shanika De Silva*
Suggested Time: 10 minutes ⏱

Focus
To encourage students to make predictions about Shanika De Silva's feelings about traditional dress and to become familiar with her voice.

Setup
Read the prediction questions out loud, and have students jot down answers as you play the introduction to the interview. Ask students to share their predictions with the class. Affirm each prediction as a possibility.

✪✪✪ LISTENING FOR MAIN IDEAS
Suggested Time: 10 minutes ⏱

Focus
To help students identify the main topics in the interview.

Setup
Read the directions, and define any new vocabulary in the exercise. Have students mark the topics while they listen. Then have students compare their answers with a partner's before checking them as a class.

✪✪✪ LISTENING FOR DETAILS
Suggested Time: 15 minutes ⏱

Focus
To help students listen for specific details in the interview.

Setup
Have students read the items and answer the ones they can. Play the interview and have students mark each statement true or false. If students seem to be having trouble, play the interview one more time. Have students compare answers with those of a partner (of different listening ability, if possible). If disagreements arise, replay those segments rather than simply giving answers.

✪✪ REACTING TO THE LISTENING
Suggested Time: 20 minutes 🕐

Focus
To encourage students to make inferences about Shanika's feelings based on tone of voice and word choice.

Setup
Read the directions. For the "Words, phrases, and tone of voice" column, explain that you want students to make notes on what Shanika says and on her tone of voice. Play Excerpt 1 while students do the task. Stop and discuss students' answers. Then play Excerpts 2–4, stopping after each excerpt to give students time to write. Replay the excerpts if necessary. As you discuss answers, welcome disagreement. Encourage students to support their ideas with details. Next, place students in small groups (of different language backgrounds, if possible) to discuss the questions in Exercise 2. Circulate among groups to listen for interesting responses to be shared with the class.

Expansion/Homework
(1) You may want to have students meet in groups (of different listening levels, if possible) to discuss their answers to the chart in Exercise 1. Then, you can have each group present a different excerpt to the class and answer any queries from their classmates. (2) The questions in Exercise 2 can be used as an audio journal assignment. Have students record their individual answers for you to review.

✪✪✪ B   LISTENING TWO: *Interview with a Fashion Designer*

Suggested Time: 15 minutes 🕐

Focus
To give students another perspective on fashion so that they can make comparisons; to give students practice listening to another voice.

Setup
Read the directions and captions in Exercise 1. Have students repeat the underlined words and guess the meaning. Affirm each guess as a possibility. Next, read the introduction to the listening, and have students circle the correct answers while they listen. Then have them compare their answers with a partner's. Go over the answers, replaying any problematic segments. Be sure to confirm their vocabulary guesses after they have completed the listening.

✪✪✪ C   LINKING LISTENINGS ONE AND TWO

Suggested Time: 20 minutes 🕐

Focus
To have students use information from both listenings to make inferences about how each speaker would react to statements about fashion.

Setup

Read the introduction and statements in the chart. Have students fill in the chart individually before sharing their answers with a partner (of a different fluency level, if possible). Call on selected students to share their ideas with the class. Allow disagreement as long as students' reasoning is sound.

Expansion/Homework

You can ask students to give their opinions of casual clothes in the workplace: *Is casual clothing acceptable in an office environment?* You can also discuss the advantages and disadvantages of wearing school uniforms: *Should students be allowed to wear casual clothing?*

Link to *NorthStar: Reading and Writing*

(1) You can ask students to consider how Shanika and Marco might respond to the following statement: *Cosmetic surgery is an effective way to look younger and more stylish.* (2) You can also bring cosmetic surgery into the discussion by asking students to consider how Shanika and Marco would react to the following statement: *It is a good idea for some people to get cosmetic surgery, color their hair, or make other cosmetic changes in order to look more like a member of a different ethnic group.* Then ask students to give examples of this and state their own opinions about it.

3 Focus on Vocabulary, PAGE 134

✪ EXERCISE 1
Suggested Time: 25 minutes

Focus

To help students understand analogies and use them to review the vocabulary of the unit.

Setup

Read the explanation and examples of analogies. Next, read the instructions to Exercise 1. Then go over the example with the whole class before dividing the class into pairs (of different fluency levels) to complete the exercise. Circulate among pairs, and offer help as needed. Then call on selected pairs to give each answer. Make sure that students are able to give explanations for each analogy.

Expansion/Homework

(1) This exercise can be assigned as homework, with class time used to review answers. (2) You can choose the best analogies for a game. Divide the class into groups of six. Read an incomplete analogy to Group 1, and have them confer before guessing the completion. If they are correct, they get a point. If not, the first group to raise their hand and answer correctly gets the point. Group 2 gets the next analogy, and the game continues.

Link to *NorthStar: Reading and Writing*

You can write vocabulary from Unit 8 on the board and ask students to create more analogies.

✪ EXERCISE 2
Suggested Time: 25 minutes 🕐

Focus

To give students a chance to guess vocabulary words based on clues provided by classmates; to review word forms (nouns and adjectives).

Setup

Read the instructions, and divide the class into small groups (of different language backgrounds, if possible). Go over the example with the whole class, and make sure students understand how the game is played. Circulate among groups and remind them to try to guess correctly using as few clues as possible. Also, remind them that clues can only be short words or phrases and that students cannot say the word on the slip of paper. Select a winning team based on which group finishes first.

Link to *NorthStar: Reading and Writing*

You can have students play the game from Exercise 2 using vocabulary words from Unit 8 of the *Reading and Writing* book.

 For extra vocabulary practice, have students work on the self-grading vocabulary activities for the unit on the NorthStar Companion Website at **http://www.longman.com/northstar**.

4 Focus on Speaking, PAGE 137

✪✪ A | PRONUNCIATION: Thought Groups

Suggested Time: 20 minutes 🕐

Focus

To give students a chance to use pauses in their speech to make it more comprehensible; to explore how the same sentence can have two different meanings based on the use of pauses.

Setup

Begin by saying the following sentence very quickly without pausing: *In the business world, it's important for men and women to dress formally.* Have the students try to repeat the sentence in a way that is easier to understand. Elicit the use of pauses, and ask them to consider when speakers should pause in a sentence. After a brief discussion, read the introduction and rules. Next, read the instructions for Exercise 1, and have the students complete it individually. Then play the audio, and have the students check their markings. Discuss any differences that arise, and reassure students that some small differences are acceptable. Then bring up the issue of how the meaning of a sentence can be changed by changing the way thought groups are presented. Have students do Exercise 2 on their own. Then read the instructions for Exercise 3, and have students complete it with a partner. Circulate among pairs to make sure they are pronouncing the sentences correctly. Then have the students repeat each sentence after you for more practice.

Expansion/Homework

(1) To check individual pronunciation, have students record the sentences in Exercise 2 in their audio journals. (2) You can have the students think of other examples of sentences with two meanings like those in Exercise 2. They can write their sentences on the board for the class to pronounce in two ways. Then the whole class can discuss how the meaning changes depending on how the thought groups are read.

✪✪✪ B STYLE: Introductions for Oral Presentations

Suggested Time: 20 minutes

Focus

To help students create interesting and informative introductions; to practice making a general topic more specific.

Setup

Give students an oral presentation topic (e.g., jeans). Elicit ways to introduce the topic, and write them on the board. Next, have students open their books, and read the suggestions and examples. Then read the list of topics, and give a few examples of making the topic more specific. Have students choose a topic, and prepare their introductions individually. Set a time limit. Next, divide the class into small groups (of different fluency levels) to present their introductions. Circulate among groups to make sure that students are predicting content as directed.

Expansion/Homework

You might choose two or three exemplary introductions to be presented to the class. After each presentation, discuss the elements that made it strong: attention grabber, specific focus, definitions.

Link to *NorthStar: Reading and Writing*

You can add cosmetic surgery to the list of oral presentation topics.

✪✪ C GRAMMAR: *Used to*

Suggested Time: 20 minutes 🕐

Focus

To have students practice using *used to*, a grammatical point that will be helpful for one of the speaking topics at the end of the unit.

Setup

If possible, bring in pictures of a celebrity (e.g., Madonna, Princess Diana), showing fashion changes throughout the years. Ask questions with *used to*, such as the following: *How did Madonna used to wear her hair? What kind of dresses did Princess Diana used to wear before she was married?* Encourage students to use *used to*, in their responses. Next, read the instructions for Exercise 1. Have students complete it and discuss the questions that follow. Then read the examples in the chart before having students work in pairs (of different fluency levels) to complete Exercise 2. Circulate among pairs to monitor their use of *used to*. Then call on individual students to share one sentence with the class. Continue until the picture has been completely described.

Expansion/Homework

(1) You can ask students to bring in one current and one old picture of themselves or a relative. Then have groups of three show their pictures, and comment on the changes that have taken place (e.g., *I used to wear dresses most of the time, but now I wear jeans. I used to have long hair, but now it's short.*) (2) To check grammatical usage, you can ask students to write six sentences comparing the two pictures for homework (after the exercise has been completed in class). Then collect the homework and make corrections. (3) For further practice, offer exercises from *Focus on Grammar, Intermediate*, and *Fundamentals of English Grammar*. See Grammar Book References on page 187 of the Student Book for specific units and chapters.

 For extra listening practice, have students use the NorthStar Companion Video.

✪✪✪ D SPEAKING TOPIC

Suggested Time: 60 minutes 🕐

Focus

To give students a chance to use the knowledge, vocabulary, and skills they have acquired to give impromptu presentations on fashion issues.

Setup
Explain what impromptu presentations are. Go over the list of suggested topics, answer any questions, and give students a few minutes to think about how each fashion item has influenced the way that people dress today. Next, divide the class into groups of six or seven students who work well together. Then read through and model the procedures for preparing and presenting the speeches. (You might want to give a sample speech.) Set up a chair and desk outside the classroom to give presenters a place to prepare. Be prepared to act as the timekeeper. Allow four minutes per presentation, if class time permits. As the students do the task, circulate among groups to make sure that students are using the Listening Task questions in their discussion.

Expansion/Homework
To help students prepare for their speeches and guide the audience's listening, you might want to prepare worksheets for the oral-presentation outline and the Listening Task.

Link to *NorthStar: Reading and Writing*
You can add cosmetic surgery to the list of oral presentation topics.

✪E   RESEARCH TOPICS

INTERPRETATION OF MAGAZINE PICTURES
Suggested Time: 60 minutes ⏲

Focus
To give students another chance to practice speaking in front of the class; to explore the connection between fashion and identity.

Setup
Bring in a sample picture of a distinctive dresser, and ask students to hypothesize about that person's personality, job, education, etc. Read the assignment, and explain the presentation procedures. As students make their presentation, make sure that audience members complete the Listening Task. Call on individual students, and ask them to state whether they agree or disagree with the speaker's interpretation. Encourage discussion of other interpretations.

Expansion/Homework
If you have a particularly shy class, you can have students present to groups of six or more students, instead of to the whole class. To create a formal presentation atmosphere, ask presenters to stand up.

Link to *NorthStar: Reading and Writing*
You can have students discuss whether or not the person in the picture may have had cosmetic surgery.

PRESENTATION ON TRADITIONAL CLOTHING
Suggested Time: 60 minutes ⊘

Focus
To give students another chance to practice oral presentation skills; to examine the theme of traditional dress.

Setup
Read the assignment. Show a picture of a person wearing traditional dress (preferably not a nationality represented in class), and do a sample presentation. Have students give presentations on their own traditional dress. Encourage them to wear the clothing during their presentations, if possible. Call on individual students to ask the speaker a follow-up question. Possible questions include: *How long does it take to make? What is it made of? Is it comfortable to wear? How much does it cost?*

Expansion/Homework
(1) If you have a mono-ethnic class, you can have each student research the traditional dress of a different culture for their presentation. (2) If students have access to PowerPoint technology, encourage them to create PowerPoint presentations for the class.

To Spank or Not to Spank?

OVERVIEW	
Theme:	Punishment

Listenings:	Listening One: *A Radio Report*
	    A report on spanking
	Listening Two: *Expert Opinions*
	    Three experts talk about spanking

Critical Thinking Skills:	Recognize personal assumptions about spanking Infer word meaning from context Identify arguments for and against spanking Evaluate persuasiveness of arguments Analyze strategies speakers use to support their opinions Compare and contrast past and current childrearing practices Develop arguments in favor of or against an issue
Listening Tasks:	Determine a speaker's point of view Identify supporting ideas Take notes using a graphic organizer Listen for details Interpret a speaker's intensity of opinion Relate listening to personal values Synthesize information from two listenings Identify end sounds Listen for specific information in student responses
Speaking Tasks:	Share background information Make predictions Make impromptu opinion statements using new vocabulary Support an opinion with facts, statistics, examples, and anecdotes Ask and answer questions Conduct a debate Express and defend opinions Use an outline to organize an argument Summarize observations on child discipline
Pronunciation:	Final consonants Tongue twisters
Vocabulary:	Word definitions Context clues Vocabulary classification
Grammar:	Present perfect tense

UNIT SUMMARY

This unit deals with the debate over the appropriateness of spanking as a punishment for children. Listening One is a radio report presenting the case of a man who was arrested for spanking his child in public. It presents both sides of the controversy from the perspective of several parents and experts. Listening Two contains more expert opinions on the topic.

The companion unit in *NorthStar: Reading and Writing* deals with the debate over capital punishment.

1 Focus on the Topic, PAGE 145

✪✪✪ A PREDICTING

Suggested Time: 5 minutes

Focus
To start students thinking about using spanking as punishment for children; to examine the meaning of the title and use it to predict the unit content.

Setup
Have students look at the picture and read the title and questions. Elicit answers to the questions from the class. Try to focus on the students' emotional reactions to the subject. Question 2 will be discussed further in the next sections.

Expansion/Homework
You may want to have partners jot down answers to the questions and compare them before the class discussion.

✪✪ B SHARING INFORMATION

Suggested Time: 20 minutes

Focus
To encourage free discussion of students' childhood experiences with punishment.

Setup
Divide the class into groups of three or four (of different language backgrounds, if possible) to answer the questions. Ask students to tell personal stories or give specific examples using the past tense.

Expansion/Homework
Since question 1 is rather personal, you may want students to discuss it in their audio journals instead of in class.

Link to *NorthStar: Reading and Writing*
You can have students discuss their ideas about the best way for a government to teach its citizens about right and wrong.

✪✪✪ C   PREPARING TO LISTEN

BACKGROUND
Suggested Time: 15 minutes 🕐

Focus
To help students learn more about attitudes toward corporal punishment.

Setup
Read the introduction to the quiz. Have students do the quiz individually. Then discuss the questions in Exercise 2 as a whole class. Encourage discussion of the quiz answers that surprised the students. Have them explain why they were surprised, and elicit cross-cultural comparisons of corporal punishment issues.

Expansion/Homework
Possible discussion questions include: *Does your home country have laws against corporal punishment? How do pediatricians in your home country feel about corporal punishment? Do you think more parents used corporal punishment in your home country in the 1950s? Do you think most parents in your home country believe that corporal punishment is the best type?* Have the students discuss these questions in small groups (of different language abilities, if possible).

VOCABULARY FOR COMPREHENSION
Suggested Time: 15 minutes 🕐

Focus
To introduce vocabulary and concepts about misbehavior and punishment in preparation for the listening.

Setup
If possible, bring in a real advice column to familiarize students with this genre. Next, have students read the letter, and match the vocabulary words with the synonyms individually before comparing their answers in pairs. Then ask pairs to exchange books and see if their answers agree. As a class, practice pronouncing the underlined words.

Expansion/Homework
To save time, you can assign the exercise as homework and use class time to work on pronunciation and check answers.

2 Focus on Listening, PAGE 148

✪✪✪ A LISTENING ONE: *A Radio Report*
Suggested Time: 10 minutes ⏲

Focus
To help students predict the opinions and speakers that will be presented in the report; to help them become familiar with the radio reporter's voice.

Setup
Have students read the prediction questions. Then play the excerpt and have students check off their predictions. Elicit the predictions, and tally them on the board. Affirm each prediction as a possibility.

✪✪✪ LISTENING FOR MAIN IDEAS
Suggested Time: 10 minutes ⏲

Focus
To get students to identify the opinions of the speakers and listen for some of the reasons.

Setup
Allow students to look at the chart. Emphasize that the most important task is listening for the speakers' opinions, but encourage them to write down as many of the reasons as they can. Play the listening once as students complete the chart. After listening, have students compare their answers with a partner before checking them as a class. Make sure students have correctly identified the speakers' opinions. You can jot some of their suggested reasons on the board, but don't review them in detail. They will be presented again in the next exercise.

✪✪✪ LISTENING FOR DETAILS
Suggested Time: 15 minutes ⏲

Focus
To help students listen for reasons for the speakers' opinions.

Setup
Have students read the items and respond to those they already know. Then play the radio report again all the way through, and have students finish the exercise and check their answers with a partner. If students seem to be having trouble, play the listening one more time. Go over the answers. If disagreements arise, replay those segments rather than simply giving the answers.

✪✪ REACTING TO THE LISTENING
Suggested Time: 25 minutes ⏲

Focus
To get students to make inferences about what the speakers think is effective parenting.

Setup

Read the introduction, making sure that students understand the two opinions. Next, read the instructions for completing the chart in Exercise 1. Then play the first excerpt, and pause to make sure students know how to respond. Continue by playing the other excerpts one at a time, and asking students to fill in the rest of the chart. Replay the excerpts as needed so students can write down specific examples from the listening to support their choices. Then discuss this exercise as a class, and be sure to welcome a variety of opinions as long as the students' reasoning is sound. For Exercise 2, divide the students into small groups (of different fluency levels, if possible) and have them discuss the questions. Call on individual students to share their answers with the whole class.

Expansion/Homework

For Exercise 2, you can divide the class into two groups (A and B) standing in lines opposite each other. Group A students move down the line and explain their opinions three times, to three different Group B students. Group B students listen and ask questions. Then the groups switch roles and repeat the activity.

✪✪✪ B LISTENING TWO: *Expert Opinions*

Suggested Time: 15 minutes 🕐

Focus

To present more opinions on the long-term effects of spanking; to give students experience with a different kind of listening.

Setup

Have students read the directions and look at the chart. Play the listening twice as students complete the chart. The first time, students can check off the speakers' opinions; the second time, they can write down the reasons. Discuss the answers as a class.

✪✪✪ C LINKING LISTENINGS ONE AND TWO

Suggested Time: 20 minutes 🕐

Focus

To encourage students to think critically by asking them to evaluate the opinions they heard in both listenings.

Setup

Read the instructions, and divide the class into small groups (of different fluency levels, if possible). Appoint a group leader to make sure that everyone has a chance to speak. Have each group make a list of the two strongest opinions on each side and prepare to explain their list to the class. Then call on each group to present its ideas. Encourage a variety of opinions as long as the reasoning is sound.

Expansion/Homework

It might be interesting to divide the students into groups of the same gender and see if there are differences in opinion.

Link to *NorthStar: Reading and Writing*

You can bring capital punishment into the discussion of child discipline by adding the following question: *If a person is abused as a child, becomes emotionally disturbed as a result, and then commits a murder when he or she is an adult, should that person be executed for his or her crime?*

3 Focus on Vocabulary, PAGE 151

✪ EXERCISE 1
Suggested Time: 25 minutes ⏱

Focus

To help students understand and practice using synonymous words and phrases; to rule out words and phrases that are not synonymous.

Setup

Read the instructions, and have the students complete the exercise individually before comparing answers with a classmate. Then call on volunteer students to read each sentence twice, using both synonymous choices. For each sentence, try to elicit other words and phrases that could be used to create the same meaning. (For example, *confessed* can be used as a synonym for *admitted* in item 5.)

Expansion/Homework

To save time, you can ask students to complete Exercise 1 as homework and be prepared to share their answers with the class.

✪ EXERCISE 2
Suggested Time: 20 minutes ⏱

Focus

To review punishment vocabulary and help students learn to use the new vocabulary items in real communication.

Setup

Read the instructions, and call on two students to demonstrate the example. Then divide students into pairs (of different fluency levels, if possible) and have them complete the exercise. Circulate among pairs, and offer correction as needed. Also, listen for good examples of word usage. Then address correction issues to the whole class and share good examples of word usage.

Expansion/Homework
This exercise can be done as a written homework exercise. Have students use items 1–7 to write sentences supporting corporal punishment. Have them use items 8–14 to write sentences opposing corporal punishment. Select some sentences for class error correction, and also for models of good usage.

Link to *NorthStar: Reading and Writing*
You can add some vocabulary from Unit 9 to this exercise. You can also challenge students to use vocabulary from both units to create a role play in which two people disagree about corporal and capital punishment. Begin the role play as follows:

STUDENT A: I think all forms of physical punishment are wrong.
STUDENT B: Do you mean that you disagree with spanking and also with capital punishment?
STUDENT A: That's right . . . (add reasons).
STUDENT B: But what about . . . (add objections).

 For extra vocabulary practice, have students work on the self-grading vocabulary activities for the unit on the NorthStar Companion Website at **http://www.longman.com/northstar**.

4 Focus on Speaking, PAGE 152

✪✪A PRONUNCIATION: Final Consonants
Suggested Time: 25 minutes

Focus
To help students hear and produce final /s/ and final /z/; to familiarize students with the vowel lengthening that takes place when nouns ending in /s/ are changed to verbs ending in /z/.

Setup
Read the introduction and the explanatory chart; model the pronunciation of the example words. Then play the audio for Exercise 1. Next, have students produce /s/ and /z/ as directed in Exercise 2. Play the audio for Exercise 3. Have students listen and repeat. Then read the instructions, and play the audio for Exercise 4. Go over the answers as a class after students have done the exercise individually. Next, read the instructions for Exercise 5, and have students complete this exercise with a partner. Then explain what a tongue twister is, and play the audio for students to listen and repeat (Exercise 6). Give students a chance to practice repeating one tongue twister individually. Call on various students to present each of the five tongue twisters. Then read the instructions for Exercise 7, and have students complete this exercise with a partner.

Expansion/Homework

(1) You can have students record all five tongue twisters in their audio journals.
(2) Another option is to play a game. First, assign each tongue twister to a pair
of students, and have them practice saying it in unison. Then have each pair
present the tongue twister to the class. Award a prize to the pair that produces
the fastest, most accurate tongue twister.

✪✪✪ B | STYLE: Supporting Your Opinions

Suggested Time: 25 minutes 🕐

Focus

To help students develop strong support for their opinions during a discussion or
debate; to prepare students for the final speaking activity of the unit.

Setup

With books closed, write the four types of support from page 154 on the board
(facts, statistics, examples, and personal stories). Ask students to define, and give
examples for, each type. Then read the explanation of support types. Next, have
students read the list of phrases that can be used to introduce support. Then
read the instructions for the small group activity. First, allow students a few
minutes to make individual notes on each discussion topic. Then divide the class
into groups (of different language backgrounds, if possible). Assign one student
to lead each discussion and to make sure that all group members express and
support their opinions. Circulate among groups to make sure that students are
providing adequate support for their opinions. Finish by having each group give
an example of the most persuasive support that was presented.

Expansion/Homework

For additional practice, you can also discuss the contexts in which each type of
support might be more appropriate. Write the following topics on the board:
Moving to a new country can be very difficult and *Immigration has greatly
increased*. Then have students discuss which type of support they would use for
each statement. Ask them to give examples of facts, statistics, examples, and
personal stories that can be used.

Link to *NorthStar: Reading and Writing*

You can use two topics related to capital punishment for this activity.

✪✪ C | GRAMMAR: Present Perfect Tense

Suggested Time: 20 minutes 🕐

Focus

To have students practice using the present perfect tense, a grammatical point
that will be used in the final speaking activity of the unit.

Setup

Discover students' existing knowledge of the grammar point by having them read the paragraph and answer the questions in Exercise 1. Then present the grammar in the explanatory chart before reading the instructions for Exercise 2. In this exercise, students should focus on using the correct verb form and spelling to complete the statements. Then have them check their answers in small groups before going over the answers as a class. For Exercise 3, students should first complete the questions with the correct verb form. Then remind them to use the present perfect, as appropriate, during their discussion. Monitor the groups to check the students' usage.

Expansion/Homework

(1) To check your students' grammatical usage, you can ask them to complete Exercises 2 and 3 in writing for homework. Then collect the papers and make corrections. (2) For further practice, offer exercises from *Focus on Grammar, Intermediate*, and *Fundamentals of English Grammar*. See Grammar Book References on page 187 of the Student Book for specific units and chapters.

For extra listening practice, have students use the NorthStar Companion Video.

✪✪✪ D | SPEAKING TOPIC

Suggested Time: 60 minutes ⏱

Focus

To give students a chance to use the knowledge, vocabulary, and skills they have acquired from the unit as they conduct a debate on corporal punishment.

Setup

Read the introduction and instructions, and divide the class into teams. Depending on your class, you can spend more or less time in class on the planning stage. In general, the more planning time students have in class, the better the debate will be. Allow students to work in groups (of different fluency levels, if possible). If possible, assign students topics that interest them and positions they agree with. As students work, move from group to group to give assistance as needed. During the debate, you can assign a time to each section of the debate so that each person has an equal chance to speak.

Expansion/Homework

(1) You may want to bring in some articles or give students time to do library/Internet research to help them find facts and statistics to support their opinions. (2) You may also want to have the audience of the debate take notes on the main points and supporting information of each team, then vote on which team presented the stronger argument. (3) You can videotape the debate and evaluate students' performances either by taking notes while showing the tape during class, or by meeting with individual students afterwards.

Link to *NorthStar: Reading and Writing*
You can use the topic of capital punishment as an example of how to plan a debate. Have students use the information they read to work in groups and plan arguments and rebuttals. Then all the arguments and rebuttals can be put on the board, and the class can critique them and assess why some are stronger than others. Alternatively, you can add another debate topic on capital punishment: *Topic 5—Capital punishment should be against the law in all countries. Some countries use capital punishment (e.g., Malaysia) and some countries do not (e.g., Great Britain).*

✪ E   RESEARCH TOPIC

OBSERVATION
Suggested Time: 15 minutes 🕐

Focus
To observe and evaluate how people in the students' environments discipline their children.

Setup
If you can, arrange an observation at a preschool, day care center, playground, or other location where students can watch children and their caretakers. Have students read the assignment, and make sure they understand it. After they have completed the observation and have made the tape recording, have students discuss their observations in small groups (of students who made different observations). Then have each group present the most interesting points to the class.

Expansion/Homework
(1) Instead of making a tape recording of their observations, students can present their results to the class or write a short report. (2) You may want to divide the class into groups, and have each group do the observation at a different location (for example, a preschool and a playground). For the discussion, group students so each group has one or more students who observed at each location. Have students discuss and compare how the discipline differed at the different locations

Before You Say "I Do"

OVERVIEW

Theme:	Marriage

Listenings:	Listening One: *A Prenuptial Agreement*
	    An interview with newlyweds
	Listening Two: *Reactions to the Prenuptial Agreement*
	    Five opinions

Critical Thinking Skills:	Interpret quotations judge the value of a prenuptial agreement Infer word meaning from context Hypothesize another's point of view Support opinion with information from the text Develop arguments for and against an issue Evaluate the quality of arguments
Listening Tasks:	Identify main ideas Listen for details Determine a speaker's point of view Identify supporting reasons Listen for emphasis in speech Listen for student interruption strategies Listen closely to interpret meaning
Speaking Tasks:	Make predictions Express and defend opinions Perform a role play using new vocabulary Use word stress to change the meaning of a sentence Practice interrupting politely Present a topic and lead a group discussion Conduct an oral history interview Research a topic and make a class presentation
Pronunciation:	Contrastive stress
Vocabulary:	Word definitions Context clues
Grammar:	Articles

UNIT SUMMARY

This unit explores the written (and unwritten) agreements couples make about their roles and responsibilities in a marriage. Listening One is an interview with a couple who wrote a prenuptial agreement detailing every aspect of their life together, from who does the shopping to what kind of food they will eat. Listening Two contains reactions from different people about the idea of a marriage agreement.

The companion unit of *NorthStar: Reading and Writing* deals with how people find a spouse in different cultures.

1 Focus on the Topic, PAGE 163

✪✪✪ A PREDICTING

Suggested Time: 10 minutes ⏲

Focus

To introduce the general topic of marriage; to discuss how a couple can have a happy marriage.

Setup

Allow students to read the questions and take notes for their answers for a minute. Then elicit the answers from the class. To encourage brainstorming, write the answers to question 3 on the board.

Expansion/Homework

Students can answer the questions in pairs (of different genders, if possible) before sharing their answers with the class.

✪✪ B SHARING INFORMATION

Suggested Time: 20 minutes ⏲

Focus

To examine quotations about marriage to explore ideas about the nature of marriage and how to have a happy one.

Setup

Read the instructions, and divide the class into small groups (of different cultural backgrounds, if possible). Circulate among the groups, and help to clarify the quotations, if needed. Then go over the answers as a class. Ask the students to explain which quotation they agree with the most.

Expansion/Homework

If students disagree with a quotation, you may want to ask them to rewrite it as a statement with which they can agree. Have students write their revised statements on the board and discuss why they disagreed with the original quotation.

✪✪✪ C PREPARING TO LISTEN

BACKGROUND
Suggested Time: 20 minutes 🕐

Focus

To introduce students to the concept of a prenuptial agreement; to give students a chance to express their opinions about prenuptial agreements.

Setup

Read the introduction, and then have individual students read the items in each section of the agreement. Then give the students a chance to discuss the questions in Exercise 2 with a partner before you call on individuals to share their ideas with the class.

Expansion/Homework

(1) For Exercise 2, you can divide the class into two groups (A and B) standing in lines opposite each other. Group A students move down the line and ask each question three times to three different Group B students. Group B students listen and answer. Then the groups switch roles and repeat the activity. (2) The second question in Exercise 2 can be used as an audio journal assignment. Have students record their answers individually, and give them your feedback.

VOCABULARY FOR COMPREHENSION
Suggested Time: 15 minutes 🕐

Focus

To introduce vocabulary related to marriage and relationships in preparation for the listening.

Setup

Ask students to read the problems and choose the best definitions for the vocabulary words. Then have students check answers as a class and practice pronouncing the vocabulary words.

Expansion/Homework

To save time, you may want to assign the exercise as homework, using class time to check answers and review pronunciation.

2 Focus on Listening, PAGE 167

✪✪✪ A   LISTENING ONE: *A Prenuptial Agreement*

Suggested Time: 15 minutes 🕐

Focus

To encourage students to make predictions about the relationship between Steve and Karen; to preview some of the questions in the interview.

Setup

Have students listen to the beginning of the interview and then read the interview questions as they listen to them. Stop the audio after each question to allow students time to write their answers. When students are finished, ask them to share their predictions with the class. Affirm each prediction as a possibility.

Expansion/Homework

Students can share their answers in a small group and then present any differences to the class for whole-class discussion. During the class discussion, encourage students to view the differences as possibilities. (Be careful not to divulge information from the listening.)

✪✪✪ LISTENING FOR MAIN IDEAS

Suggested Time: 10 minutes 🕐

Focus

To help students listen for the problems of marriage discussed in the interview.

Setup

Have students read the list of problems before they listen. Play the interview only once. Then have students compare their answers with a partner or with the class. If possible, allow students to correct each other, rather than relying on you for the correction.

✪✪✪ LISTENING FOR DETAILS

Suggested Time: 15 minutes 🕐

Focus

To help students listen for specific details about the content of the marriage agreement.

Setup

First have students read the items and answer the ones they already know. Then play the interview again all the way through. Allow students to compare their answers with a partner or with the class. If there is a lot of disagreement, replay the report, stopping after the confusing parts for discussion and clarification.

✪✪ REACTING TO THE LISTENING
Suggested Time: 20 minutes ⏱

Focus
To encourage students to make inferences about the couple's opinions about marriage by comparing their statements to the quotations about marriage from Section 1B.

Setup
Have students read the questions. They may first want to review the quotations in Section 1B. Then play the excerpts from the interview, and allow students time after each one to answer the questions. Replay the excerpts as needed so students can write down specific examples from the listening to support their opinions. Discuss the answers as a class. Then have students do Exercises 2 and 3 in small groups.

Expansion/Homework
You may want to divide students into groups (of different listening levels, if possible) and let them answer the questions together.

Link to *NorthStar: Reading and Writing*
You can ask students to discuss the following questions: *What do you think about having parents help couples write prenuptial agreements? What do you think about having prenuptial agreements include a rule about "group marriage" (being married to more than one person)?*

✪✪✪ B ▌ LISTENING TWO: *Reactions to the Prenuptial Agreement*
Suggested Time: 15 minutes ⏱

Focus
To present different reactions to Steve and Karen's prenuptial agreement; to give students practice listening to other speakers.

Setup
Read the instructions and have students read the list of reasons. Then play the listening. You may want to play it twice. The first time students can check off Good idea or Bad idea, and the second time they can match the speaker with the reason for his or her opinion. Have students exchange books to compare answers.

Expansion/Homework
You can ask students to state which reason makes the most sense to them. You can also ask them to add their own reasons for considering a prenuptial agreement to be a good or bad idea.

✪✪✪ C LINKING LISTENINGS ONE AND TWO

Suggested Time: 15 minutes ⏱

Focus

To allow students to react to Steve and Karen's prenuptial agreement; to explore the strongest arguments for and against prenuptial agreements.

Setup

Read the instructions and have the students complete Exercise 1 in pairs (of the same gender, if possible). Encourage use of the vocabulary from Section 1C by writing it on the board. Then call on each pair to present their choices to the class. If there is heated debate, encourage it. Insist, however, that students be respectful of each others' customs and beliefs.

Expansion/Homework

You can have students prepare a role play in which one partner wants to write a prenuptial agreement and the other partner does not. Have them use arguments in this section in their role play. Give students time to prepare in class, and then call on student volunteers to perform their role play for the class.

3 Focus on Vocabulary, PAGE 170

✪ EXERCISE 1

Suggested Time: 15 minutes ⏱

Focus

To use context clues to figure out the meaning of scrambled words; to review vocabulary from the unit.

Setup

Do the first item as an example. Next, have students do the rest individually. Then go over the answers together.

Expansion/Homework

This exercise can be done as homework.

✪ EXERCISE 2

Suggested Time: 20 minutes ⏱

Focus

To figure out a saying about marriage using letters from the words in Exercise 1.

Setup

Read the instructions, and make sure the students know how to proceed. Have them complete the exercise individually. Then write the complete saying on the board, and discuss its meaning.

Expansion/Homework

(1) This exercise can be done as homework. (2) You can turn this activity into a game by setting a time limit, and awarding a small prize to the student who finishes first.

✪ EXERCISE 3
Suggested Time: 30 minutes

Focus

To give students a chance to use vocabulary from the unit in a role-play activity.

Setup

Read the instructions, and divide the class into small groups (of different fluency levels, if possible). Next, provide containers (such as envelopes), and have each group select three words as directed. Then have each group select one role-play situation. Circulate among groups as they prepare the role plays, making sure that each group member has a speaking part. Then have each group perform its role play. Remind students in the audience to write down the vocabulary words that they hear.

Expansion/Homework

(1) You can challenge students to use more than three words, or to use each word more than once. (2) To avoid repetition, you can assign role-play situations to each group, or give students the option of creating their own.

Link to *NorthStar: Reading and Writing*

You can have students use vocabulary from Unit 10 of the *Reading and Writing* book to create a role play.

 For extra vocabulary practice, have students work on the self-grading vocabulary activities for the unit on the NorthStar Companion Website at **http://www.longman.com/northstar**.

▌**4** ▌ Focus on Speaking, PAGE 173

✪✪ A ▌ PRONUNCIATION: Contrastive Stress

Suggested Time: 20 minutes

Focus

To develop an ability to use and understand contrastive stress when it is used to add new information or contradict previous information.

Setup

Write *I usually wash the dishes.* on the board. Say the sentence four times, stressing a different word each time. Ask students to identify the words you stress and how the meaning changes. Have students open their books and study the chart describing contrastive stress. For Exercise 1, play the audio, and have students circle the implied meaning. Stop after the first item to make sure that students understand the exercise and that they are doing it correctly. Check the answers as a class. For Exercise 2, read the example out loud to show how to pronounce the first sentence with both meanings. Then divide students into pairs (of different language backgrounds, if possible) to do the exercise. Walk around the room to monitor and correct pronunciation of the contrastive stress as they practice. Then read the instructions for Exercise 3, and have students complete it with the same partner.

Expansion/Homework

You can have volunteer pairs stand in front of the class and read their sentences from Exercise 3. Ask the class to explain the meaning of each sentence.

✪✪✪ B | STYLE: Interrupting Politely

Suggested Time: 25 minutes 🕐

Focus

To practice ways of politely interrupting someone in order to speak during a group discussion or conversation; to prepare for the final speaking activity of the unit.

Setup

With students' books closed, put the headings *Body Language* and *Words/Phrases* on the board. Have students give their own ideas about body language and words or phrases that can be used to interrupt. Then look at the chart in the book, and compare it with the ideas of the class. Read and discuss the explanatory information accompanying the chart. Divide students into groups of three or four (of different fluency levels, if possible) for Exercise 1. After students have prepared for discussion, read the instructions for Exercise 2. For each group, appoint a "listener" to keep track of the interrupting. After the discussion, ask the students how they felt interrupting and being interrupted. Reassure them that this is a polite and effective way to communicate in English.

Expansion/Homework

You can provide additional practice by giving students a chance to interrupt you politely while you are speaking to the class. First, explain that is culturally acceptable for speakers of American English to interrupt teachers as long as it is done politely. Next, appoint a record keeper to keep track of how many times students are able to interrupt you politely. Then begin speaking on a simple, familiar topic (e.g., nuclear family structure). After this activity, discuss the strategies that students used to interrupt you, and how they felt about using them.

Link to *NorthStar: Reading and Writing*
You can add the following topic to the discussion activity in Exercises 1 and 2:
What is the best way to find a spouse?

✪✪ C   GRAMMAR: Articles

Suggested Time: 20 minutes 🕒

Focus

To have students practice using definite and indefinite articles (*the, a/an*), a grammatical point that will be used in the final speaking activity of the unit.

Setup

Have students read the excerpt from the prenuptial agreement and answer the questions. Next, ask them to explain the rules they know for using articles. Then have them refer to the explanatory chart for clarification. Next, read the instructions for Exercise 2, and explain how changing an article can change the meaning of a sentence. Have students do the matching activity. Then read the instructions for Exercise 3, and model the pronunciation of the sentences in item 1. Have students complete the exercise with a partner. Circulate among pairs and monitor their work. Remind students that they need to have accurate pronunciation for their partner to get the correct answer.

Expansion/Homework

(1) You may want to have students work in pairs to write sentences and meanings similar to those in Exercise 2. Have students put their sentences on the board. Discuss any errors, and then have the class discuss the different meanings. (2) For further practice, offer exercises from *Focus on Grammar, Intermediate*, and *Fundamentals of English Grammar*. See Grammar Book References on page 187 for specific units and chapters.

✪✪✪ D   SPEAKING TOPIC

Suggested Time: 60 minutes 🕒

Focus

To give students a chance to use the knowledge, vocabulary, and skills they have acquired from the unit to present information to classmates and lead a discussion.

Setup

Read the directions. Divide students into groups of four or five students. Give students time to write their outlines, following the example. Then have students take turns presenting their topics and leading discussion. Circulate among groups to make sure students are asking open questions and giving participants a chance to speak. Allow 6–10 minutes per presentation, if class time permits.

Expansion/Homework

(1) If you have a small class, you might want to have students present their topics to the class. Review strategies for interrupting politely, and encourage students to use them while they listen. (2) To save class time, you can have students prepare their outlines at home.

⭐E RESEARCH TOPICS

ORAL HISTORY
Suggested Time: 10 minutes ⏱

Focus

To have students listen to and retell the story of a couple's first meeting and courtship.

Setup

Review the assignment with the students. Help them identify a couple to interview. It is not necessary for the interviews to be conducted in English; the reporting task is more important. You may want to select a few of the best tapes to play for the whole class.

Expansion/Homework

In lieu of preparing a tape, the students can work in small groups (of classmates who work together well) to share information about the stories that they heard.

RESEARCH AND DISCUSSION
Suggested Time: 30 minutes ⏱

Focus

To help students find out more about a marriage topic through research; to allow students to lead a discussion about their topic.

Setup

Have students pick a topic. Review important tips for conducting library and/or Internet research. Have students do their research for homework, using the questions as a guide. Encourage students to write down extra information in addition to the answers to the questions. Have students present and discuss their information in small groups (of students who chose different topics).

Expansion/Homework

Instead of small group discussions, you can have students present their information in short oral presentations. After each presentation, give students individual feedback in note form on the content, delivery, and accuracy (pronunciation and grammar) of their presentation.

Link to *NorthStar: Reading and Writing*

You can broaden the research focus to include different courtship customs, including those mentioned in the reading text (e.g., arranged marriage, group marriage).

Student Book Answer Key

UNIT 1

VOCABULARY FOR COMPREHENSION, page 4

1. d	4. c	7. g	10. f
2. a	5. e	8. i	
3. b	6. h	9. j	

LISTENING FOR MAIN IDEAS

1 page 5

Emotional Appeals	Products Advertised
humor	flea collar
ego	hair color

2 page 5

1. b
2. a
3. b

LISTENING FOR DETAILS, page 6

1. b	4. b	7. b	10. a
2. c	5. a	8. a	
3. a	6. c	9. c	

B LISTENING TWO, page 8

Thief Buster ad—c
Rinse Away ad—a

3 FOCUS ON VOCABULARY

1 page 9

1. products
2. guilty
3. embarrassed
4. ad
5. specialize
6. fit
7. techniques
8. persuade

A PRONUNCIATION

1 page 11

1. Kathy: Hello?
   Liz: (Kathy)! I took your (advice).
   Kathy: (What) advice?
   Liz: I colored my (hair).
   Kathy: With Younger (You)?
   Liz: (Yes)! It's (great)!
2. Kathy: Did you hear about that new (flea) collar?
   Liz: (Yes), I'm going to the pet store (today). How about (you)?
   Kathy: I think I'll stop by (tomorrow).

B STYLE

1 page 13

1. d	2. c	3. a	4. b

C GRAMMAR

1 page 14

"Don't delay. Get a Doggie's Friend today."

UNIT 2

VOCABULARY FOR COMPREHENSION, page 21

1. a	4. a	7. a	10. b
2. b	5. b	8. c	
3. c	6. c	9. a	

LISTENING FOR MAIN IDEAS, page 23

1. T	3. T	5. T
2. F	4. F	6. F

LISTENING FOR DETAILS, page 23

1. b	4. a	7. a	10. b
2. a	5. b	8. b	
3. b	6. c	9. a	

B LISTENING TWO, page 25

1. a	2. b	3. b	4. a

3 FOCUS ON VOCABULARY

1 page 26

1. ascent
2. summit
3. diagonally
4. climb
5. steep
6. experience
7. deceiving
8. ridge
9. plant
10. rhythm
11. goal
12. sensation

A PRONUNCIATION

2 page 28

1. reach
2. pen
3. mess
4. sit
5. reason
6. men
7. fail
8. pet
9. seat
10. sick

4 page 29

a. a deep breath
   a steep ascent
b. sensation seekers
   my favorite people
c. windy weather
   a little rest
d. risk takers
   the thrill of danger
e. keep the rhythm
   a steep hill

C GRAMMAR

1 page 30

Dave: <u>Would you prefer</u> . . . <u>would you rather</u>

Jennifer: <u>I'd rather not</u>

Dave: <u>Would you prefer</u>

Jennifer: <u>I prefer</u> . . . <u>I'd rather</u>

UNIT 3

B SHARING INFORMATION

1 page 38

2. **Sweepstakes scam:** when someone gets you to pay money for a prize that doesn't exist
3. **Medical fraud:** when someone sells medical products or services that don't work
4. **Internet fraud:** when someone uses the Internet to sell you a product that doesn't exist

VOCABULARY FOR COMPREHENSION, page 40

a. 5	d. 6	g. 10	j. 2
b. 3	e. 9	h. 7	
c. 1	f. 4	i. 8	

A LISTENING ONE

1 page 41

1. b   2. c   3. a

LISTENING FOR MAIN IDEAS, page 41

Order of steps: 2, 3, 5, 4, 1

LISTENING FOR DETAILS, page 42

1. c	4. b	7. b	10. a
2. c	5. a	8. c	
3. a	6. b	9. a	

B LISTENING TWO, page 44

1. d   2. b   3. a   4. c

3 FOCUS ON VOCABULARY

1 page 45

1. victim / con artist
2. sweepstakes / prize
3. criminals / crimes
4. protect / put pressure on
5. trusted / reassured
6. deposit / payment
7. scam / trick
8. gullible / excited
9. rob /swindle
10. fraud / theft

A PRONUNCIATION

2 page 48

A: going to (gonna)

B: have to (hafta)

A: have to (hafta), want to (wanna)

B: want to (wanna)

A: have to (hafta)

B: has to (hasta)

A: have to (hafta)

B: going to (gonna)

C GRAMMAR

1 page 50

1. as bad as
2. worse than
3. not as dangerous as, less trusting than

UNIT 4

VOCABULARY FOR COMPREHENSION

1 page 58

1. g	3. c	5. b	7. e
2. f	4. a	6. h	8. d

2 page 58

1. f	3. a	5. d
2. e	4. c	6. b

LISTENING FOR MAIN IDEAS, page 60

1. a girl, Lavender
2. his coat
3. to her house, home
4. back to Lavender's house
5. she was a ghost

LISTENING FOR DETAILS, page 60

a. 2	c. 1	e. 7	g. 3
b. 6	d. 5	f. 4	

B LISTENING TWO

1 page 62

1. c   2. b   3. a

3 FOCUS ON VOCABULARY

1 page 63

1. date		6. chilled
2. lavender		7. driveway
3. wore on		8. headlights
4. strict		9. picket fence
5. fell on		10. weeds

A PRONUNCIATION

1 page 65

1. from
2. on
3. with
4. to
5. in
6. at
7. to
8. for

2 page 66

1. d
2. e
3. c
4. a
5. f
6. b

C GRAMMAR

1 page 68

1. to
2. base form
3. Why?

2 page 69

1. e
2. c
3. a
4. d
5. b

UNIT 5

C PREPARING TO LISTEN

2 page 75

1. b
2. c
3. a

VOCABULARY FOR COMPREHENSION, page 75

1. a
2. a
3. b
4. a
5. b
6. a
7. b
8. b
9. b
10. b

LISTENING FOR MAIN IDEAS, page 77

1. c
2. a
3. c

LISTENING FOR DETAILS, page 78

1. b
2. c
3. c
4. a
5. a
6. b

B LISTENING TWO, page 79

Code switching = changing <u>from one way of talking to another</u>

Ex: One dialect at <u>home</u>
   Another dialect at <u>school or work</u>

Gotta bounce = <u>I've got to leave.</u>
the crew = <u>my friends</u>
phat gear = <u>nice clothes</u>

Teens speak differently because <u>(1) they want to show their identity and to show they fit in with friends; (2) to show that they are separate from their parents.</u>

3 FOCUS ON VOCABULARY

1 page 80

1. became aware
2. commented on
3. self-conscious
4. stereotyped
5. bright
6. fit in
7. slang
8. intentionally
9. accepted
10. identity

A PRONUNCIATION

1 page 83

1. can't
2. can
3. can't
4. can
5. can't
6. can't
7. can
8. can

C GRAMMAR

1 page 86

1. The first and second sentences are about past events.
2. The third and fourth sentences are about the present.
3. The fifth and sixth sentences are about the future.

UNIT 6

VOCABULARY FOR COMPREHENSION, page 94

a. 3
b. 1
c. 2
d. 4
e. 5
f. 7
g. 6
h. 10
i. 8
j. 9

LISTENING FOR MAIN IDEAS, page 96

1. b
2. a
3. c
4. b

LISTENING FOR DETAILS, page 96

1. F
2. F
3. T
4. T
5. F
6. F
7. T
8. T
9. T

REACTING TO THE LISTENING

2 page 97

Sandra supports the attraction:

- It helps preserve their tradition.
- It provides long-necked women with money.

Fredrick opposes the attraction:

- It is a dead tradition.
- It is degrading to the women.

B LISTENING TWO, page 99

1. c
2. a
3. a
4. b

A PRONUNCIATION

1 page 101

/əd/—invited, ended, visited, attracted

/t/—helped, stretched, wrapped, talked

/d/—harmed, allowed, improved, rubbed

3 page 102

1. talked
2. wrapped
3. stretched
4. attracted
5. improved
6. allowed
7. invited
8. ended

C GRAMMAR

1 page 103

1. eight past tense verbs: went, drove, relaxed, went (swimming), ate, learned, didn't buy, took
2. verbs ending with -ed = regular verbs; other verbs = irregular verbs

UNIT 7

BACKGROUND, page 112

1. The punch line is "Climb a tree and act like a nut." "Nut" has two meanings: (1) a large seed; (2) a person who behaves strangely.
2. A fence goes around a house but doesn't move.
3. The answer to "Knock-knock" is "Who's there?" The pun is "ketchup."
   "Ketchup" (tomato sauce) sounds like "catch up" (hurry up).
4. The group or profession is firefighters. The joke says that firefighters can make simple jobs complicated.

VOCABULARY FOR COMPREHENSION, page 112

1. a
2. b
3. b
4. a
5. b
6. a
7. b
8. b
9. a
10. a

A LISTENING ONE, page 114

1. a radio talk show
2. a sociologist
3. Answers will vary.

LISTENING FOR MAIN IDEAS, page 114

1. To help people deal with problems; To help people to bond to each other
2. Pun; Lawyer joke

LISTENING FOR DETAILS, page 114

1. a
2. a
3. c
4. b
5. b
6. a
7. a
8. a
9. b
10. a

B LISTENING TWO, page 116

Joke 1: h
Joke 2: d
Joke 3: g
Joke 4: f
Joke 5: b
Joke 6: e
Joke 7: c
Joke 8: a

C LINKING LISTENINGS ONE AND TWO

1 page 117

Joke 1: a
Joke 2: d
Joke 3: c
Joke 4: b
Joke 5: c
Joke 6: a
Joke 7: b
Joke 8: d

3 FOCUS ON VOCABULARY

1 page 118

Across

2. offensive
3. punch line
5. category
7. socialize
8. make fun
9. riddle
11. solidarity
15. humor
16. give up

Down

1. comedy
4. cartoon
6. deal with
10. comic
12. ironic
13. ancient
14. bond

A PRONUNCIATION

2 page 120

1. Is he home?
2. Tell her I'm here.
3. Call him today.
4. Write her a letter.
5. Tell his mother to come.

C GRAMMAR

1 page 123

1. Jerry Seinfeld
2. New York
3. comedian

2 page 123

1. Who, Where, What. They are all *wh-* question words.
2. information questions

3 page 124

Student A—Questions

1. When was Jerry Seinfeld born?
2. Where did he study after high school? / Where did he go to college?
3. Who kept the money but didn't send light bulbs?
4. Why was Jerry invited to perform on two famous late-night talk shows?
5. Who is Jerry married to?
6. Who feels that life is just about perfect?

Student A—Answers for blanks

1. April 29, 1954
2. Queens College
3. Jerry's boss
4. he was so popular
5. Jessica Sklar
6. Jerry

Student B—Questions

1. Who was born on April 29, 1954?
2. What city was Jerry born in? / Where was Jerry born?
3. What did Jerry sell over the phone?
4. How did Jerry become a star?
5. What was his TV show called? / What was the name of his TV show?
6. Who is Sascha?

Student B—Answers for blanks

1. Jerry
2. New York
3. light bulbs
4. He began telling jokes at a comedy club.
5. Seinfeld
6. daughter

UNIT 8

VOCABULARY FOR COMPREHENSION, page 129

1. h	4. i	7. f	10. e
2. g	5. a	8. j	
3. d	6. b	9. c	

A LISTENING ONE, page 130

1. Los Angeles, California
2. Answers will vary.

LISTENING FOR MAIN IDEAS, page 130

Topics mentioned: 1, 2, 4, 6, 7, 8, 10

LISTENING FOR DETAILS, page 130

1. T	4. T	7. F	10. T
2. T	5. T	8. F	
3. F	6. F	9. T	

B LISTENING TWO

1 page 132

polo shirt = short sleeved, dressy t-shirt with a collar

casual = informal

sweater = warm, long sleeved shirt made of knitted yarn

stylish = fashionable

2 page 132

1. c	3. b	5. a
2. b	4. a	6. c

3 FOCUS ON VOCABULARY

1 page 135

1. old-fashioned. The opposite of practical is impractical. The opposite of modern is old-fashioned.
2. sarong or sari. You put on pants. You wrap a sarong or sari.
3. sari. A man wears a sarong. A woman wears a sari.
4. modern. A sari is traditional. Jeans are modern.
5. jeans. Coke is a kind of soft drink. Levi's are a kind of jeans.
6. casual. The opposite of strong is weak. The opposite of formal is casual.
7. handbag. You wear a sarong. You carry a handbag.
8. comfortable. High heels are uncomfortable. Athletic shoes are comfortable.

A PRONUNCIATION

1 page 137

1. It's a long piece of cloth that's wrapped around your waist.
2. They're great for formal occasions, but if you're hanging out with friends, you want something more modern.
3. . . . family background can influence the way you dress.
4. The men, I guess, used to wear a sarong.
5. . . . when I was a kid growing up in Sri Lanka, I didn't wear saris.
6. But now that I'm older, I like to wear saris sometimes.

2 page 138

1. a–d, b–c	4. a–c, b–d
2. a–d, b–c	5. a–d, b–c
3. a–c, b–d	6. a–c, b–d

C GRAMMAR

1 page 140

1. used to wear, used to feel. The speaker uses *used to* to show that the actions were repeated in the past but don't happen anymore.
2. The speaker doesn't use *used to* because Shanika still knows the value of traditional clothing and still wears saris for special occasions.

UNIT 9

BACKGROUND, page 146

Answers are in Student Activities, page 185 of the Student Book.

VOCABULARY FOR COMPREHENSION, page 147

a. 5	d. 11	g. 9	j. 7
b. 8	e. 1	h. 3	k. 2
c. 4	f. 10	i. 6	

LISTENING FOR MAIN IDEAS, page 148

1. Supports. Pain is necessary to teach children right from wrong; Spanking is done out of love.
2. Opposes. Spanking teaches children to fear their parents; Spanking teaches children that problems should be solved with violence.
3. Supports. Spanking is sometimes the best way to get a child's attention.
4. Opposes. Spanking can lead to more violent behavior in children; Children who are spanked usually misbehave more than other children.

LISTENING FOR DETAILS, page 149

1. Y	4. Y	7. N
2. N	5. N	8. Y
3. N	6. Y	9. N

B LISTENING TWO, page 150

1. Opposes. Violent criminals were almost always spanked as kids; Corporal punishment teaches children to be violent.
2. Supports. Teenagers in a study did better with clear discipline, like spanking; Spanking doesn't hurt if it's done in a loving home.
3. Supports. Spanking is decreasing but violent crime is increasing; Corporal punishment is one way for parents to control their children.

3 FOCUS ON VOCABULARY

1 page 151

Crossed out words:

1. pleased with	6. wrong
2. yell at	7. reward
3. reward	8. love
4. prevents	9. agree to
5. denied	10. do well

A PRONUNCIATION

1 page 153

1. /z/
2. /s/

4 page 153

abuse (verb)	rice
lose	plays
peace	niece
ice	advise
fears	race

C GRAMMAR

1 page 155

1. have/has + past participle
2. when a past action continues today or has current relevance
3. when a past action began and ended in the past

2 page 156

1. have changed; have stopped
2. has passed; have arrested
3. have advised; have suggested
4. has risen; have not taught
5. have stopped; has decided

3 page 157

1. have . . . changed
2. has . . . passed
3. have . . . advised
4. Has . . . risen . . . fallen
5. has . . . changed

UNIT 10

B SHARING INFORMATION, page 164

1. a
2. b
3. a

VOCABULARY FOR COMPREHENSION, page 166

a. 2	d. 5	g. 10	j. 7
b. 4	e. 3	h. 6	
c. 1	f. 8	i. 9	

LISTENING FOR MAIN IDEAS, page 167

Problems mentioned: 1, 3, 5, 6

LISTENING FOR DETAILS, page 168

1. F	3. F	5. T	7. T
2. T	4. F	6. F	8. T

B LISTENING TWO, page 169

Speaker 1: Bad idea—c

Speaker 2: Bad idea—d

Speaker 3: Good idea—a

Speaker 4: Bad idea—e

Speaker 5: Good idea—b

3 FOCUS ON VOCABULARY

1 page 170

1. bothers
2. work out
3. compromise
4. occur
5. agreement
6. break
7. check on
8. concern
9. expectations
10. quirks
11. spend time
12. legal

2 page 172

All marriages are happy. Living together afterwards is difficult.

A PRONUNCIATION

1 page 174

1. a
2. b
3. b
4. a
5. a
6. b
7. a
8. b
9. b
10. a

3 page 175

1. (Steve's). . . twice, (Karen's). . . once
2. (Many). . . money, (a few). . . other situations

3. (Steve). . . car, (Karen). . . housework
4. (Married). . . easy, (living). . . difficult
5. (Karen). . . early, (Steve). . . late
6. (Steve). . . Japanese, (Karen). . . Mexican
7. (One couple). . . marriage, (other couple). . . divorce
8. (Most). . . verbal, (few). . . written

C GRAMMAR, page 177

1. nouns, adjectives
2. *a/an* = indefinite (not specific); *the* = definite (specific)

2 page 178

1. a–d, b–c
2. a–d, b–c
3. a–c, b–d
4. a–d, b–c
5. a–d, b–c
6. a–c, b–d
7. a–d, b–c
8. a–c, b–d

Unit Word List

The **Unit Word List** is a summary of key vocabulary from the Student Book's Vocabulary for Comprehension and Focus on Vocabulary sections. The words are presented by unit, in alphabetical order.

Unit 1

ad
appeal (noun)
effective
ego
embarrassed
embarrassment
emotion
emotional appeal
fear
fit (verb)
guilt

guilty
humor
humorous
luxury (adjective)
manipulate
persuade
product
romance
specialize
target market
technique

Unit 2

ascent
axe (noun)
climb
dangerous
deceiving
diagonally
experience (noun)
extreme
feeling
frightened
frightening

goal
plant (verb)
push the limits
rhythm
ridge
sensation
steep
strong
summit
tired

Unit 3

angry
cheat
cheerful
con artist
confident
crime
criminal
deposit (noun)
excited
fraud
frustrated
gullible
joyful
lose
luxury
payment
pleased
prize (noun)

protect oneself
put pressure on
reassure
reassured
rob
scam
scared
surprised
sweepstakes
swindle
telemarketing
theft
trick (verb)
trust (verb)
unsure
victim
worried

Unit 4

approach
cemetery
chilled
date (noun)
driveway
fall on
gravestone
headlight

lavender
picket fence
shy
social (noun)
strict
wear on
weed (noun)

Unit 5

accent
accept someone
aware
become aware of
bright
code switch
comment on (verb)
dialect
fit in

identity
intelligent
intentionally
regional
self-conscious
slang
social
standard
stereotype (verb)

Unit 6

aspect
attraction
collarbone
controversial
controversy
degrading
discomfort
farmer
harm (verb)
harmful
mayor
negative
neutral

oppose
popular
positive
preserve (verb)
souvenir
stretched
support (verb)
tourism
tourist attraction
tradition
wrapped
zoo

Unit 7

ancient
bond (verb)
cartoon
category
comedy
comic strip
deal with
give up
humor
ironic
irony
joke
make fun of
offensive
pun
punch line
riddle
sense of humor
socialize
society
solidarity

Unit 8

athletic shoes
attitude
be in style
casual
comfortable
designer
exotic
formal
handbag
hang out
high heels
influence (verb)
jeans
miniskirt
model (noun)
modern
occasion
offbeat
old-fashioned
pants
polo shirt
practical
sari
sarong
shorts
style
stylish
sweater
tend to
traditional
trendy
T- shirt
unique
value (noun)
Western

Unit 9

acceptable
admit
agree with
angry at
arrest
child abuse
complain
corporal punishment
deny
discipline (verb)
for one's own good
get in trouble
lead to
misbehave
pleased with
punish
respect (verb)
reward (verb)
spank
support (verb)
upset with
violence
yell at

Unit 10

agreement
bother (verb)
break the rules
check on
compromise (noun)
concern (verb)
disagree
expectation
get married
legal
marriage
marry
occur
prenuptial agreement
quirk
romantic
spend time
wedding
work out

Introduction to Achievement Tests

The following reproducible Achievement Tests allow teachers to evaluate students' progress and to identify any areas where the students might have problems in developing their listening and speaking skills. The Achievement Tests should be given upon completion of the corresponding Student Book unit.

Description   There are two Achievement Tests for each unit. **Test 1** is a "paper and pencil" test of receptive skills. It assesses students' mastery of listening comprehension and of the vocabulary, pronunciation, and grammar points introduced in the unit.

Test 2 is intended to assess the students' productive, or speaking, skills. It consists of a speaking task related to the content of the unit. Each speaking task is designed to elicit a speech sample lasting several minutes.

Administration   Administration of **Test 1** requires use of the recorded material on the audio CD packaged with this Teacher's Manual. Students will need to listen to the audio program in order to answer the questions in each section of the test. The answer key to the tests and the audioscript of the material on the CD are included at the end of the Achievement Test section.

Teachers can decide how to incorporate **Test 2** (the speaking task) into their testing situations. Some teachers will assign each speaking task immediately after students complete **Test 1**; others may decide to set aside another time to complete it. The tasks may be set up for pairs, small groups, the whole class, or on a teacher-to-student basis. When set up for pairs or small groups, teachers will need to circulate around the classroom and spend enough time with each pair or group to evaluate the production of individual students.

Some teachers may not find it possible to evaluate all of the students on every speaking test. As an alternative, teachers may choose to evaluate only part of a class on a given **Test 2** speaking task and evaluate the remaining students on tests given at a later time. Teachers may also choose to evaluate students only on every other test or on a total of three or four tests over the term.

Scoring Test 1   Individual test items are worth one point, for a maximum total of 30 points per test. To facilitate scoring, an answer key is provided at the end of the book. A student's score can be obtained by adding together the number of correct items. To obtain an overall "listening score" for a student, teachers may average all of the **Test 1** scores that the student received in the class.

Scoring Test 2   Speaking tasks are evaluated holistically using the categories in the rating sheet that follows. The categories include content, vocabulary, pronunciation, and grammar. In each category, 0 indicates poor or inadequate performance for the level; 1 indicates average or acceptable performance; 2 indicates good or outstanding performance. The teacher circles the rating for each category and adds the numbers to obtain a total score out of 8 possible points.

Test 2 Rating Sheet

Student: _____ Unit _____

Content	0	1	2
Vocabulary	0	1	2
Pronunciation	0	1	2
Grammar	0	1	2

Total Score _____

The teacher can complete the rating sheet for each student's test and give it to the student. It can also be kept by the teacher as a record of each student's progress.

An overall "speaking score" for a student may be obtained by averaging all of the **Test 2** scores the student received in the class.

Achievement Tests
Unit 1

Name: _____

Date: _____

TEST 1

A. ☐**1** *Listen to the excerpt. Mark the main ideas **T** (true) or **F** (false).*

The Thief Buster system can keep someone from _____.

_____ **1.** touching your car

_____ **2.** entering your car

_____ **3.** driving away with your car

☐**2** *Listen again. What does the speaker say about the Thief Buster security system? Check the details that apply.*

_____ **1.** It's inexpensive.

_____ **2.** It can be used to protect houses.

_____ **3.** It's completely effective.

_____ **4.** It has an alarm.

B. *Listen to each sentence and identify the correct answer.*

_____ **1.**   **a.** make someone do something

_____ **2.**   **b.** control

_____ **3.**   **c.** match

_____ **4.**   **d.** do one thing very well

_____ **5.**   **e.** something that makes us interested

_____ **6.**   **f.** what we think of ourselves

_____ **7.**   **g.** ways of doing things

_____ **8.**   **h.** a way to make us laugh

_____ **9.**   **i.** full of feeling

_____ **10.**   **j.** ashamed or uncomfortable

_____ **11.**   **k.** high standard and expensive

C. *Listen for the highlighted word in each sentence. Circle the highlighted word below.*

1. are / you

2. I'm / terrible

3. what / happened

4. job / interview

5. go / on

6. saw / dandruff

7. couldn't / concentrate

D. *Read the suggestions below. Then listen to the problems. Find one positive suggestion and one negative suggestion to match each problem.*

Positive Suggestions

a. Help him with his homework.
b. Start an exercise program.
c. Get it repaired.
d. Call the police.
e. Turn off more lights.

Negative Suggestions

f. Don't light your house while you're not at home.
g. Don't drive it anymore.
h. Don't argue with them about it.
i. Don't let him miss classes.
j. Don't eat so much food.

Problems

1. positive suggestion _____   negative suggestion _____

2. positive suggestion _____   negative suggestion _____

3. positive suggestion _____   negative suggestion _____

4. positive suggestion _____   negative suggestion _____

5. positive suggestion _____   negative suggestion _____

TEST 2

Talk about an advertisement you like or dislike.

• What is the ad selling?

• What emotional appeal does the ad use?

• Is the ad successful?

• Why do you like or dislike the ad?

Achievement Tests
Unit 2

Name: _____

Date: _____

TEST 1

A. **1** *Listen to part of an interview with a world-famous skateboarder. Mark the main ideas* **T** *(true) or* **F** *(false).*

The skateboarder _____.

_____ 1. thinks his real career is more important than skateboarding

_____ 2. tries hard to get things right

_____ 3. learns new tricks quickly and easily

2 *Listen to the interview again. Check all the topics mentioned.*

_____ 1. the skateboarder's trip to France

_____ 2. his reason for going to France

_____ 3. the year of the Summer X Games

_____ 4. the amount of time it took him to perfect the 900

_____ 5. the skateboarder's daily routine

B. *Listen to each sentence and circle the correct answer.*

1. **a.** the top of a mountain   **b.** the climb up a mountain

2. **a.** go at an angle   **b.** go straight up

3. **a.** you did recently   **b.** you want to do

4. **a.** easy   **b.** difficult

5. **a.** you can't do it   **b.** you can hardly do it

6. **a.** you can't trust   **b.** you think is exciting

7. **a.** a high point   **b.** a rocky area

8. **a.** while singing   **b.** in a regular pattern

9. **a.** the top   **b.** the end

10. **a.** feel   **b.** wish

C. *Listen to the sentences and the pairs of words. Circle the correct vowel pattern in the stressed syllables.*

      1. **a.** /ɪ/—/ɛ/   **b.** /iy/—/ɪ/

      2. **a.** /iy/—/ɛ/   **b.** /ey/—/iy/

      3. **a.** /ɪ/—/ɛ/   **b.** /iy/—/ɪ/

      4. **a.** /ey/—/iy/   **b.** /ɛ/—/ɪ/

      5. **a.** /ey/—/ɪ/   **b.** /ey/—/iy/

      6. **a.** /iy/—/ey/   **b.** /ɪ/—/ey/

      7. **a.** /iy/—/ey/   **b.** /ɪ/—/ey/

 D. *Listen to each conversation. Then circle the correct answer.*

      1. **a.** She'd rather hike.   **b.** She'd rather ski.

      2. **a.** He wants to go swimming.   **b.** He doesn't want to go swimming.

      3. **a.** He prefers tennis.   **b.** He prefers golf.

      4. **a.** She wants to stay home.   **b.** She wants to go out.

      5. **a.** She'd rather rest.   **b.** She'd rather not rest.

TEST 2

Describe a situation in which you had to push your limits.

- What was the situation?
- Why was it challenging?
- How did you feel?

Achievement Tests
Unit 3

Name: _____

Date: _____

TEST 1

A. **1** *Listen to the story. What happened? Number the events in the correct order (1–4).*

Anne _____.

_____ sent in the money

_____ called the number in the ad

_____ saw a newspaper ad

_____ received the drinks

2 *Listen to the story again. Mark the details **T** (true) or **F** (false).*

_____ 1. Anne got a job as a flight attendant.

_____ 2. Anne sent in $3,000.

_____ 3. She lost a lot of weight.

_____ 4. She didn't speak with Mr. Zimmerman.

B. *Listen to each sentence and circle the correct answer.*

1. **a.** a swindler   **b.** a victim

2. **a.** part of the money   **b.** all of the money

3. **a.** something you buy   **b.** something you win

4. **a.** doubt what someone says   **b.** believe what someone says

5. **a.** try to make someone do something   **b.** make it hard for someone to do something

6. **a.** ready to believe what people say   **b.** not ready to believe what people say

7. **a.** keep yourself from harm   **b.** try not to worry about something

C. *Listen to the people talk about how they feel. Circle the best answer to complete the sentences.*

   1. **a.** worried   **b.** happy

   2. **a.** embarrassed   **b.** frustrated

   3. **a.** excited   **b.** guilty

   4. **a.** unsure   **b.** reassured

   5. **a.** angry   **b.** frightened

 D. *Listen to the sentences. Are the words below reduced or not reduced? Check (✓) the correct answers in the chart.*

	Reduced	Not Reduced
1. have to		
2. going to		
3. wants to		
4. going to		
5. have to		
6. want to		

 E. *Each of the sentences you will hear contains a comparative or an equative. Listen and circle the correct answers.*

   1. **a.** comparative   **b.** equative

   2. **a.** comparative   **b.** equative

   3. **a.** comparative   **b.** equative

   4. **a.** comparative   **b.** equative

TEST 2

Give your opinion about this statement: "Telephone con artists are as bad as bank robbers."

• Do you agree or disagree with this statement?

• Why do you agree or disagree with it?

Achievement Tests
Unit 4

Name: _____

Date: _____

TEST 1

A. ☐1 *Listen to the interview with Jackie Torrence. Mark the main ideas **T** (true) or **F** (false).*

According to Jackie, a storyteller should _____.

_____ 1. practice reading a story several times

_____ 2. like a story that he or she tells

_____ 3. only talk about his or her own family

☐2 *Listen to the interview again. Check (✓) the things that Jackie talks about.*

_____ 1. the age of the storyteller

_____ 2. the characters in a story

_____ 3. the length of the story

_____ 4. the language in a story

B. *Listen to each sentence and circle the correct answer.*

1. **a.** a kind of cloth   **b.** a color

2. **a.** to go slowly   **b.** to go quickly

3. **a.** the lights in front   **b.** the lights in back

4. **a.** you have many rules   **b.** you don't have rules

5. **a.** cold   **b.** wet

6. **a.** something to wear   **b.** someone to go with

7. **a.** a party   **b.** an interview

8. **a.** a marker where someone is buried   **b.** a place where many people are buried

9. **a.** a road that goes to a house   **b.** a wide, open road

10. **a.** fruit trees   **b.** wild, unwanted plants

11. **a.** a low, open fence   **b.** a tall, solid wall

12. **a.** to leave   **b.** to come near

C. *Listen to the sentences. Circle the preposition that you hear in each sentence.*

     1. **a.** in   **b.** at

     2. **a.** on   **b.** in

     3. **a.** from   **b.** for

     4. **a.** to   **b.** at

     5. **a.** in   **b.** on

     6. **a.** of   **b.** in

 D. *A friend is asking John about his evening at a social. First, read John's answers below. Then listen to the friend's questions. Match each question with the correct answer.*

Questions	**John's Answers**
_____ 1.	I did that _____.
_____ 2.	**a.** to be sure that I wouldn't get chilled
_____ 3.	**b.** in order not to arrive home late
_____ 4.	**c.** in order to get to know her better
_____ 5.	**d.** to see if I could meet someone there
	e. to find out why a friend hadn't come

TEST 2

Talk about the importance of storytelling in your family.

- Did people tell you stories when you were a child?
- Where and when did they tell you stories?
- What did you learn from the stories?

Achievement Tests
Unit 5

TEST 1

🎧 **A.** ☐1 *Listen to the excerpt. Mark the main ideas **T** (true) ar **F** (false).*

_____ **1.** Using different dialects at home and at work is an example of code switching.

_____ **2.** Teenage slang is a kind of dialect.

_____ **3.** By using teen slang with friends, a teenager is saying to them, "I'm different from you."

🎧 ☐2 *Listen to the excerpt again. Check all of the topics mentioned.*

_____ **1.** dialect used at school

_____ **2.** slang words used by teens

_____ **3.** slang used by teachers

_____ **4.** parents' reactions to teen slang

_____ **5.** teens' way of dressing

_____ **6.** teens' sense of identity

🎧 **B.** *Listen to each sentence and circle the correct answer.*

   1. a. try to learn something   **b.** suddenly know something

   2. a. say something about it   **b.** do something about it

   3. a. will think of you   **b.** will do in the future

   4. a. speaks a different language   **b.** acts a certain way

   5. a. a smart person   **b.** a slow person

   6. a. similar to them   **b.** better than them

   7. a. the standard dialect   **b.** an informal dialect

   8. a. it's easier   **b.** you want to

   9. a. dislike it   **b.** think it's OK

  10. a. you like   **b.** you are

C. *Listen to the following sentences. Circle* **can** *or* **can't.**

1. (*Can/Can't*) you tell me about your background?

2. I (*can/can't*) speak Russian.

3. She (*can/can't*) remember when she was a child.

4. We (*can/can't*) accept that.

5. Other people (*can/can't*) make me feel self-conscious.

6. Bill (*can/can't*) speak in different accents.

7. (*Can/Can't*) you hear me?

8. They (*can/can't*) use teenage slang.

 D. *Listen to the sentences with* **can** *and* **could.** *Circle the correct meaning for each sentence.*

1. **a.** past   **b.** present   **c.** future

2. **a.** past   **b.** present   **c.** future

3. **a.** past   **b.** present   **c.** future

4. **a.** past   **b.** present   **c.** future

5. **a.** past   **b.** present   **c.** future

TEST 2

Give advice to someone who is unhappy about his or her accent in English.

- Is it OK to have an accent?

- What can someone do to change his or her accent?

Achievement Tests
Unit 6

Name: _____

Date: _____

TEST 1

A. 　 **1** *Listen to the excerpt. Mark the main ideas **T** (true) or **F** (false).*

_____ 1. The scientist's job is to study the effects of tourism.

_____ 2. He is seeing more tourists in Antarctica than he used to.

_____ 3. There aren't enough tourists there to harm the environment.

2 *Listen again. Check all of the things the scientist talks about.*

He talks about _____.

_____ 1. how long he's been in Antarctica

_____ 2. a 1989 oil spill

_____ 3. the effects of global warming

_____ 4. plants and animals in Antarctica

_____ 5. how many tourists he sees each year

B. *Listen to each sentence and circle the correct answer.*

1. **a.** something you've been doing for a long time **b.** something you just started to do

2. **a.** a good feeling **b.** a painful feeling

3. **a.** making someone feel ashamed **b.** making someone feel afraid

4. **a.** a place people like to visit **b.** a place people try to avoid

5. **a.** to spread something **b.** to keep something

6. **a.** something people agree with **b.** something people disagree about

7. **a.** things to remember a place **b.** things to send to your friends

C. *Listen to the words. Is each word positive, negative, or neutral? Check (✓) the correct answers in the chart.*

	Positive	Negative	Neutral
1.			
2.			
3.			
4.			
5.			
6.			

D. *Listen to the sentences and the regular verbs in the past tense. In the chart, check the correct pronunciation for each verb.*

	/əd/	/t/	/d/
1.			
2.			
3.			
4.			
5.			
6.			

 E. *Listen to the questions. Complete the answers with the past tense form of the verbs you hear.*

1. He _____ to Hawaii.

2. He _____ there by plane.

3. He _____ a room near the beach.

4. He _____ some beautiful Hawaiian shirts.

5. He _____ over $3,000.

TEST 2

Talk about a place you have visited that is popular with tourists.

- What is the place?

- Why do tourists go there?

- How did you feel about the presence of tourists there?

- Was your visit a positive or a negative experience? Explain.

Achievement Tests
Unit 7

Name: _____

Date: _____

TEST 1

A. **1** *Listen to the excerpt. What did Jerry do? Put the main ideas in the correct order* **(1–4).**

_____ He worked at a comedy club.

_____ He won an Emmy award.

_____ He sold light bulbs and jewelry.

_____ He performed on late-night talk shows.

2 *Listen again and check all the details that are mentioned.*

_____ **1.** Jerry Seinfeld's birthplace

_____ **2.** the name of his high school

_____ **3.** his parents' background

_____ **4.** the name of the comedy club where he worked

_____ **5.** the year he won an Emmy award

B. *Listen to each sentence and identify the correct answer.*

_____ **1.**   **a.** the funny statement at the end of a joke

_____ **2.**   **b.** a joke that uses a word with two meanings

_____ **3.**   **c.** the ability to say or do funny things

_____ **4.**   **d.** to get close to someone

_____ **5.**   **e.** to stop trying

_____ **6.**   **f.** to laugh at someone

_____ **7.**   **g.** very old

_____ **8.**   **h.** funny because something doesn't make sense

_____ **9.**   **i.** rude and upsetting

C. *Listen to the sentences. Write the missing words in the blanks.*

1. _____ know I'm coming?

2. You'd better _____ your question.

3. We _____ some money.

4. _____ friend right now.

5. _____ name?

6. They _____ a joke.

D. *Read the questions below and listen to the answers. Identify the answer that goes with each question.*

Questions	Answers
1. How is your mother?	_____
2. Which book is mine?	_____
3. Where were you born?	_____
4. Who was that?	_____
5. What time did you get up?	_____
6. What does she do?	_____

TEST 2

Talk about your favorite kind of humor.

• What kind of humor is it? (puns, slapstick, riddles, knock-knock jokes, etc.)

• Why do you like this kind of humor?

• What is an example of this humor?

Achievement Tests
Unit 8

Name: _____

Date: _____

TEST 1

A. **1** *Listen to the interview. Choose the best answer to complete each main idea.*

1. Abdullah is talking about _____.
   a. traditional clothing
   b. clothing to sleep in
   c. women's clothing

2. People wear this style of clothing because _____.
   a. it looks more businesslike
   b. it shows they respect their culture
   c. it costs less than other kinds

2 *Listen to the interview again. Check the details that are mentioned.*

_____ 1. a description of a *dishdasha*

_____ 2. a description of a *quitra*

_____ 3. the color of a *quitra*

_____ 4. the cost of traditional clothing

_____ 5. for what occasions men wear this clothing

_____ 6. what kind of clothing women wear

B. *Listen to each sentence and circle the correct answer.*

1. **a.** to do it a lot   **b.** to do it very little

2. **a.** comfortable   **b.** unusual

3. **a.** useful   **b.** useless

4. **a.** to work there   **b.** to relax there

5. **a.** to wear fashionable clothes   **b.** to wear traditional clothes

6. **a.** different   **b.** delicious

7. **a.** something useful   **b.** something cool

8. **a.** to surprise   **b.** to affect

9. **a.** expensive   **b.** fashionable

10. **a.** the way someone thinks   **b.** what someone does

C. *Listen to the sentences. Circle the number of thought groups you hear in each sentence.*

1.   1   2   3
2.   1   2   3
3.   1   2   3
4.   1   2   3
5.   1   2   3
6.   1   2   3

D. *Listen to what each person says. Complete each sentence with **used to** or **didn't use to**.*

1. He _____ play tennis.

2. She _____ go to the theater.

3. He _____ use e-mail.

4. She _____ wear a sari.

5. He _____ drink milk.

6. She _____ think about fashion.

TEST 2

Talk about the importance of fashion in your life.

- Do you like to wear stylish clothes?
- Do you spend a lot of money on clothes?
- Do you think it is important to dress well? Why or why not?

Achievement Tests
Unit 9

TEST 1

A. **1** *Listen to a mother talk about spanking. Then read the main ideas below. Write **M** to identify the mother's opinions and **F** to identify the father's opinions.*

_____ 1. Spanking is a form of child abuse.

_____ 2. Spanking is a type of punishment.

_____ 3. Spanking can help teach a child about right and wrong.

_____ 4. Spanking can lead to more serious problems.

2 *Listen again and mark the details **T** (true) or **F** (false).*

_____ 1. The mother and father don't agree about discipline.

_____ 2. She never feels like spanking her children.

_____ 3. She believes in talking with her children about their problems.

_____ 4. Her husband thinks that she doesn't really punish their children.

B. *Listen to the people talk about disciplining children. Circle the best word or phrase to complete each opinion.*

1. **a.** good   **b.** right
2. **a.** spanking   **b.** punishment
3. **a.** abuse me   **b.** respect me
4. **a.** misbehave   **b.** trouble
5. **a.** parents   **b.** criminals
6. **a.** harmful   **b.** acceptable
7. **a.** discipline   **b.** support
8. **a.** admit it   **b.** explain it
9. **a.** get into trouble   **b.** learn right from wrong
10. **a.** complain about it   **b.** support it

C. *Listen to the sentences and the words. Circle the word you hear in each sentence.*

1. a. peace   b. peas
2. a. race   b. raise
3. a. place   b. plays
4. a. price   b. prize
5. a. niece   b. knees
6. a. bus   b. buzz

 D. *Listen to the sentences. Are they in the present perfect or another tense? Check (✓) the correct answers in the chart below.*

	Present Perfect	Another Tense
1.		
2.		
3.		
4.		
5.		
6.		

TEST 2

Talk about this statement: "Parents should never spank their children."

- Do you agree or disagree with the statement?
- When is spanking OK?
- When is spanking not OK?

Achievement Tests
Unit 10

Name: _____

Date: _____

TEST 1

A. ☐1 *Listen to the excerpt and mark each main idea **T** (true) or **F** (false).*

_____ 1. When they got married, the couple had different ideas about cleaning.

_____ 2. They reached a compromise, but they weren't happy about it.

☐2 *Listen again. Circle the best answer to complete the details.*

1. Before they were married, he used to _____.
   a. clean his apartment himself   **b.** pay someone to clean his apartment

2. At first the husband expected her _____.
   a. to do all the cleaning   **b.** to share the cleaning with him

3. Now they _____.
   a. usually go out for dinner   **b.** share the cooking equally

4. Now he does _____.
   a. half the cleaning   **b.** most of the cleaning

5. Before they could agree, they had to _____.
   a. get other people's advice   **b.** talk about the problem a lot

B. *Listen to each sentence and circle the correct answer.*

1. **a.** something strange or funny   **b.** something attractive

2. **a.** what happened to them   **b.** what they thought would happen

3. **a.** to satisfy   **b.** to upset

4. **a.** to be about   **b.** to comment on

5. **a.** to follow the rules   **b.** to ignore the rules

6. **a.** to help them   **b.** to get information about them

7. **a.** people who are in love   **b.** people who are friends

8. **a.** to understand   **b.** to solve

9. **a.** you can use it in court   **b.** it can help your relationship

10. **a.** disagreement   **b.** agreement

C. *Listen to each sentence. Underline the word that is emphasized. Then circle the correct meaning.*

1. Karen will take care of meals.

   a. not Steve   **b.** not the garden

2. We agree to share chores inside the house.

   a. not outside the house   **b.** not inside the garage

3. We will exercise and eat healthy food.

   a. not just exercise   **b.** not junk food

4. Steve will wash the clothes.

   a. not Karen   **b.** not dry them

5. On weekdays we will wake up by 6 A.M.

   a. not weekends   **b.** not by 7 A.M.

6. We will both make a grocery list.

   a. together, not separately   **b.** not another kind of list

7. We will spend 15 minutes talking with each other.

   a. not 5 minutes   **b.** not arguing

 D. *Listen to each sentence. Circle the correct response.*

1. **a.** I don't know the restaurant.   **b.** I know the restaurant.

2. **a.** We know what the present was.   **b.** We don't know what the present was.

3. **a.** It was one of their arguments.   **b.** It was the same old argument.

4. **a.** We've seen the house.   **b.** We haven't seen the house.

5. **a.** We know the friend.   **b.** We don't know the friend.

6. **a.** I know the name of the paper.   **b.** I don't know the name of the paper.

TEST 2

Talk about this quote: "Marriage is like life—it is a field of battle, and not a bed of roses." (Robert Louis Stevenson—adapted)

• What does this quote mean?

• Do you agree or disagree with it? Explain.

Achievement Tests
Test 1 Audioscript

UNIT 1

A

1 Listen to the excerpt. Mark each sentence **T** (true) or **F** (false).

You park your car, and your worst nightmare happens! When you come back . . . it's gone! It can happen anywhere . . . and chances are, one day, it will happen to *you*! That's why you need the incredible Thief Buster security system. It's easy to use and 100 percent effective. If someone so much as touches your car, an alarm will ring. And if that doesn't stop the thief, the engine will turn off when he tries to drive the car. So why put your car at risk any longer? Get a Thief Buster security system today! Thief Buster . . . protection for your peace of mind!

2 Listen again. What does the speaker say about the Thief Buster security system? Check the details that apply.

B

Listen to each sentence and identify the correct answer.

1. Some clothing stores <u>specialize</u> in selling fashionable, high-quality clothes, while others <u>specialize</u> in selling less expensive, everyday clothes. To <u>specialize</u> means to _____.
2. The boat was very expensive, and the setting of the ad was a beautiful home on the beach, so the ad <u>fit</u> the product very well. To <u>fit</u> means to _____.
3. The salesman was very good, so he <u>persuaded</u> me to buy the books he was selling. To <u>persuade</u> someone means to _____.
4. Advertisers try to <u>manipulate</u> our feelings through their ads. To <u>manipulate</u> is to _____.
5. The ad made me laugh, so I remembered the product. I think ads that use <u>humor</u> can be very effective. <u>Humor</u> is _____.
6. There are many <u>techniques</u> that painters use to create art. For example, they may paint unusual shapes or use special colors. <u>Techniques</u> are _____.
7. Advertisements use different kinds of <u>appeals</u> to get people's attention. An <u>appeal</u> is _____.
8. People want to feel important, so another way to sell something is to involve their <u>egos</u>. <u>Egos</u> are _____.
9. My friend lives in a <u>luxury</u> apartment with a swimming pool, an exercise room, and a beautiful garden. <u>Luxury</u> is _____.
10. The politician made an <u>emotional</u> speech. <u>Emotional</u> is when someone or something is _____.
11. I wore jeans to a fancy party. I was so <u>embarrassed</u>. When you are <u>embarrassed</u>, you are _____.

C

Listen for the highlighted words in each sentence. Circle the highlighted word below.

1. Brad, how are you?
2. I'm terrible.
3. Why? What happened?
4. Well, I had a job interview, and . . .
5. Yes. Go on.
6. The boss saw my dandruff.
7. I just couldn't concentrate.

D

Read the suggestions below. Then listen to the problems. Find one positive suggestion and one negative suggestion to match each problem.

1. My car keeps breaking down.
2. My son is failing at school.
3. My electric bills are too high.
4. My neighbors are very noisy late at night.
5. I've gained a lot of weight recently.

UNIT 2

A

1 Listen to part of an interview with a world-famous skateboarder. Mark the main ideas **T** (true) or **F** (false).

Interviewer: Let's start with the high point of your career. Can you pick out one to share with us?

Tony Hawk: Oh yes, definitely. For me, the high point came when I was traveling to France and I had to fill out a tourist information card. You know, the thing you fill out when you're entering a new country? Well, I got to write down "skateboarder" as my occupation. How cool.

Interviewer: You mean that was better than what you accomplished at the 1999 Summer X Games?

TH: You mean landing the 900? That was awesome, too. But that was pure obsession—story of my life. Nothing new for me there.

Interviewer: How was landing that trick an obsession for you?

TH: Well, like everything else I do on a skateboard, I have to get it right. It took me thirteen years of practice to perfect the 900, and on that day, I think it took me something like twelve times before I made it.

Interviewer: Did you really work on one trick for thirteen years? That does seem like an obsession!

2 *Listen to the interview again. Check all the topics mentioned.*

B _____

Listen to each sentence and circle the correct answer.

1. We started the <u>ascent</u> early in the morning. <u>Ascent</u> means _____.
2. At first we went <u>diagonally</u> across the mountain. To go <u>diagonally</u> means to _____.
3. Our <u>goal</u> was to get to the top by noon. A <u>goal</u> is something _____.
4. The climb was very <u>steep</u>. A <u>steep</u> climb is _____.
5. I was <u>pushing my limits</u> on this climb. To <u>push your limits</u> means _____.
6. The mountain was <u>deceiving</u>. <u>Deceiving</u> is something that _____.
7. We got to a <u>ridge</u>, but we weren't at the top. A <u>ridge</u> is _____.
8. We kept walking <u>in rhythm</u>. <u>In rhythm</u> means _____.
9. Finally, we made it to the <u>summit</u>. <u>Summit</u> means _____.
10. It was a great <u>sensation</u>. A <u>sensation</u> is something you _____.

C _____

Listen to the sentences and the pairs of words. Circle the correct vowel pattern in the stressed syllables.

1. We **reached** the **ridge**. Reached / ridge
2. I took a **deep breath**. Deep / breath
3. I need a **little rest**. Little / rest
4. Was the **weather windy**? Weather / windy
5. Some people are **sensation** seekers. Sensation / seekers
6. They like the **thrill** of **danger**. Thrill / danger
7. They're **risk takers**. Risk / takers

D _____

Listen to each conversation. Then circle the correct answer.

1. **Man:** Would you rather hike or ski?
   Woman: I prefer hiking.
2. **Woman:** Would you like to go swimming today?
   Man: I'd rather not.
3. **Woman:** Do you like tennis?
   Man: Well, I prefer it to golf.
4. **Man:** What do you want to do tonight?
   Woman: I'd rather stay home than go out.
5. **Man:** What would you prefer, to rest or to keep climbing?
   Woman: Let's rest for a minute.

UNIT 3

A _____

1 *Listen to the story. What happened? Number the events in the correct order (1–4).*

Hi, my name is Anne. I'm depressed because I recently lost a lot of money. Here's what happened. I wanted to get a job as a flight attendant on an airplane. The problem was that I had to lose ten pounds within one week to be able to get the job. It seemed impossible. Then I saw an ad in the newspaper for a quick weight-loss product. It seemed too good to be true! The ad said I could lose fourteen pounds in one week. I was so excited because I thought I would be able to lose the weight and get the job.

The quick weight-loss product was a drink. The man who discovered the drink was John Zimmerman. Mr. Zimmerman was offering a special price for one month only. The treatment would cost only $2,000 instead of $3,000. I sent in the $2,000 and received the drinks. I took the drinks for a week but I didn't lose any weight at all. When I tried to call the number in the ad, I found out the phone had been disconnected. The whole business was a fraud. The drink didn't work, and Mr. Zimmerman didn't exist.

2 *Listen to the story again. Mark the details **T** (true) or **F** (false).*

B _____

Listen to each sentence and circle the correct answer.

1. Yesterday someone called Jacob and asked him to send money. Jacob realized he was a <u>con artist</u>, so he hung up the phone. What is a <u>con artist</u>?
2. The furniture was expensive, so I gave the store a <u>deposit</u> of $500. What is a <u>deposit</u>?
3. Carol entered a contest, and she won a big <u>prize</u>. What is a <u>prize</u>?
4. Bob's girlfriend lied to him, so he doesn't <u>trust</u> her anymore. What does <u>trust</u> mean?
5. I didn't want to buy the insurance, but the salesman <u>put pressure on</u> me until I gave in. What does <u>put pressure on</u> mean?
6. We didn't believe Carl's story about all the money he won at the races. We aren't that <u>gullible</u>. What does <u>gullible</u> mean?
7. I tried to <u>protect myself</u> from the cold weather by wearing a heavy coat. What does <u>protect yourself</u> mean?

C _____

Listen to the people talk about how they feel. Circle the best answer to complete the sentences.

1. My daughter is hiking in the mountains this weekend. Yesterday the weather was fine, but today it's stormy and cold. I hope she's all right, but I feel _____.

2. My car keeps breaking down. Every week it seems there's a new problem, and I have to take it in to be repaired. I'm getting very _____.
3. I'm going to Spain next week. I've always wanted to go there so I'm feeling really _____.
4. I heard my husband was in an accident but he called and told me he was all right. So now I'm feeling _____.
5. I was a victim of telemarketing fraud last year. When I think about all these con artists trying to cheat people out of their money, I get _____.

D _____

Listen to the sentences. Are the words below reduced or not reduced? Check the correct answers in the chart.

1. We have to leave now.
2. I'm gonna take your picture.
3. She wants to get a free vacation.
4. We're going to Hawaii soon.
5. You hafta send a deposit.
6. We wanna win the sweepstakes.

E _____

Each of the sentences you will hear contains a comparative or an equative. Listen and circle the correct answers.

1. Fraud victims are often more trusting than most people.
2. Shoplifters are as dishonest as car thieves.
3. Telephone con artists are harder to catch than bank robbers.
4. Lying to a friend is as bad as lying to your boss.

UNIT 4

A _____

1️⃣ *Listen to the interview with Jackie Torrence. Mark the main ideas **T** (true) or **F** (false).*

Stasio: You have an interesting technique that you recommend for storytelling, for learning a story. And that is to read it five times before you tell it. Why is that?

Torrence: Yes. Well, the first time you tell a story, you see that you like it. And I always say don't ever tell a story you don't like, 'cause you've wasted your time and the time of your listener.

Then the second time you read, read it for the pictures. Read it for the pictures that you're going to create. As you read about the characters, you read a personality into those characters. You give those characters a look, you see them as familiar individuals. They may look like your husband, your wife, your daughter, your son.

The third time you read it, read it for the words. Now this is a very important part of the story, because words make that story. You can make it or break it by saying the right or wrong words.

2️⃣ *Listen to the interview again. Check the things that Jackie talks about.*

B _____

Listen to each sentence and circle the correct answer.

1. The girl wore a <u>lavender</u> dress to the dance. She looked beautiful. <u>Lavender</u> is _____.
2. We stayed up all night to study for the test. As the night <u>wore on</u>, we got more and more tired. To <u>wear on</u> means _____.
3. As I was driving along the road, I suddenly saw the <u>headlights</u> of another car. <u>Headlights</u> are _____.
4. Donna's parents are a little <u>strict</u>. They don't let her go out alone at night, and they expect her to be home by 9 P.M. <u>Strict</u> means _____.
5. You'd better not go outside in this stormy weather. You might get <u>chilled</u>. <u>Chilled</u> is _____.
6. All my friends are going to the party on Saturday night, but I don't have a <u>date</u>. A <u>date</u> is _____.
7. He invited me to the <u>social</u>, but I couldn't go. A <u>social</u> is _____.
8. Clara saw her dead uncle's name on the <u>gravestone</u>. A <u>gravestone</u> is _____.
9. I walked along the <u>driveway</u>, which was cracked and had grass growing on it. A <u>driveway</u> is _____.
10. Betty had a beautiful garden last year, but now it is full of weeds. <u>Weeds</u> are _____.
11. John's garden has a <u>picket fence</u> in front of it to keep out the animals. A <u>picket fence</u> is _____.
12. As I <u>approached</u> the highway, I realized that I needed some gas. To <u>approach</u> is _____.

C _____

Listen to the sentences. Circle the preposition that you hear in each sentence.

1. They were waiting at the house.
2. The car was parked in the driveway.
3. This package is for David.
4. Jack pointed to the house.
5. What's in the desk?
6. I'm not afraid of the dark.

D _____

A friend is asking John about his evening at a social. First, read John's answers below. Then listen to the friend's questions. Match each question with the correct answer.

1. Why did you go to the social alone?
2. Why did you take your overcoat?
3. Why did you call someone while you were there?
4. Why did you dance with one person all night?
5. Why did you leave early?

UNIT 5

A

1 *Listen to the excerpt. Mark the main ideas **T** (true) or **F** (false).*

Today I want to talk about "code switching." Code switching is when a person switches, or changes, from one way of talking to another. Usually, it happens in different situations. So, a person may use one dialect at home, and then code switch to another dialect at school or work.

One example of code switching is the way teenagers change their speech when talking to their friends or to an adult. You've probably experienced this as a teenager—there were some slang words that you used only with your friends, not with parents or teachers. And your parents probably hated the way you spoke, right? Parents always hate teen slang. But anyway, this slang, it's really a teenage dialect. And when teens switch from the teen dialect to the standard dialect, this is code switching.

. . . Why do teenagers use this dialect? Well, because it's an important way for teens to show their identity—to show that they fit in with their friends. It also shows that they are separate from their parents. So by code switching into a teenage dialect with their friends, a teenager is saying, "I'm one of you."

2 *Listen to the excerpt again. Check all of the topics mentioned.*

B

Listen to each sentence and circle the correct answer.

1. After coming to the United States, Peter <u>became aware</u> he had an accent. To <u>become aware</u> means to _____.
2. He noticed his accent because many people <u>commented on</u> it. To <u>comment on</u> something means to _____.
3. Their comments made him feel <u>self-conscious</u>. To feel <u>self-conscious</u> means to feel worried about what others _____.
4. He knew that other people <u>stereotyped</u> him because of the way he spoke. To <u>stereotype</u> means to think that a person _____.
5. He could tell that they thought he wasn't very <u>bright</u> because he talked slowly. A <u>bright</u> person is _____.
6. In college, Peter wanted to <u>fit in</u> with other students. To <u>fit in</u> with other people means to be _____.
7. He tried to speak like his friends by using <u>slang</u> when he talked. <u>Slang</u> is _____.
8. Peter's accent changed, but not <u>intentionally</u>. To do something <u>intentionally</u> is to do it because _____.
9. Peter's friends at International House <u>accepted</u> his accent. To <u>accept</u> something means to _____.
10. Peter feels that his accent is part of his <u>identity</u>. Your <u>identity</u> is the kind of person _____.

C

*Listen to the following sentences. Circle **can** or **can't**.*

1. Can you tell me about your background?
2. I can't speak Russian.
3. She can't remember when she was a child.
4. We can accept that.
5. Other people can't make me feel self-conscious.
6. Bill can speak in different accents.
7. Can't you hear me?
8. They can use teenage slang.

D

*Listen to the sentences with **can** and **could**. Circle the correct meaning for each sentence.*

1. Now I can send e-mail on my computer.
2. A few years ago I couldn't use a computer.
3. However, I still can't do a lot of other things.
4. I can take another computer class next semester.
5. I could work with computers after I graduate.

UNIT 6

A

1 *Listen to the excerpt. Mark the main ideas **T** (true) or **F** (false).*

As a scientist working in Antarctica, I spend most of my time in the lab studying ice. Today, as with an increasing number of days, I had to leave my work to greet a group of tourists who were taking a vacation here. When tourist groups visit, they take us away from our research. In addition, tourists in Antarctica can hurt the environment because they leave trash on beaches and disturb the plants and animals. In a place as frozen as Antarctica, it can take 100 years for a plant to grow back, and tourists taking pictures of baby penguins may not pay close attention to what their feet are stepping on. Oil spills are another problem caused by tourism. In 1989, one cruise ship caused an oil spill that killed many penguins and destroyed a five-year scientific project.

2 *Listen again. Check all of the things the scientist talks about.*

B

Listen to each sentence and circle the correct answer.

1. Mark and Sally go out for dinner on New Year's Eve. It's a <u>tradition</u> for them. What is a <u>tradition</u>?
2. After exercising for an hour, I felt some <u>discomfort</u> in my legs. What does <u>discomfort</u> mean?
3. It's <u>degrading</u> to have to beg for a living. What does <u>degrading</u> mean?
4. The old city had become a big <u>attraction</u> for tourists. What is an <u>attraction</u>?
5. They're trying to <u>preserve</u> their language by teaching it in school. What is <u>preserve</u>?

6. There's a lot of <u>controversy</u> about the new plan to bring more tourists to our community. What does <u>controversy</u> mean?
7. While I was on vacation on the tropical island, I bought some <u>souvenirs</u>. What are <u>souvenirs</u>?

C _____

Listen to the words. Is each word positive, negative, or neutral? Check the correct answers in the chart.

1. attraction
2. harm
3. coil
4. improve
5. popular
6. painful

D _____

Listen to the sentences and the regular verbs in the past tense. In the chart, check the correct pronunciation for each verb.

1. A friend **invited** me to come to her house last weekend. **Invited**
2. It was cold, so I **wrapped** myself in warm clothing. **Wrapped**
3. I **stayed** at her house for several hours. **Stayed**
4. We **talked** about everyone we knew. **Talked**
5. After a while, we stood up and **stretched**. **Stretched**
6. Our visit **ended**, and I drove back home. **Ended**

E _____

Listen to the questions. Complete the answers with the past tense form of the verbs you hear.

1. Where did Robert go on vacation?
2. How did he get there?
3. What did he rent?
4. What did he buy?
5. How much did he spend on his trip?

UNIT 7

A _____

1 *Listen to the excerpt. What did Jerry do? Put the main ideas in the correct order (1–4).*

Jerry Seinfeld was born on April 29, 1954, in the city of New York. He grew up in Brooklyn, and after high school he studied at Queens College.

One of Jerry's earliest jobs was to call people over the phone to sell them light bulbs. When people sent in money, Jerry's boss kept it, but didn't send any bulbs. In another job, Jerry sold cheap jewelry on the street and pretended it was expensive.

This dark period in Jerry's life did not last long. He began telling jokes at a comedy club called Catch a Rising Star, and that is how he became a star himself.

Later, he was invited to perform on two famous late-night talk shows because he was so popular. And before long he had his own TV show called "Seinfeld." The show was so successful that he won an Emmy award in 1993 for Best Comedy Show. Since then he was won many other awards.

2 *Listen again and check all the details that are mentioned.*

B _____

Listen to each sentence and identify the correct answer.

1. My friend loves <u>puns</u> because he enjoys playing with language. A <u>pun</u> is _____.
2. When I listened to the joke, I didn't understand the <u>punch line</u>. A <u>punch line</u> is _____.
3. Barbara enjoys good jokes and has a wonderful <u>sense of humor</u>. A <u>sense of humor</u> is _____.
4. I felt hurt when my friends <u>made fun of</u> me. To <u>make fun of</u> means _____.
5. I went to a movie with a new friend, and we laughed at the same jokes. It helped us <u>bond</u> as friends. To <u>bond</u> is _____.
6. That's it. I don't understand your joke. I <u>give up</u>. To <u>give up</u> means _____.
7. I'm a lawyer, and I find it <u>offensive</u> when people tell jokes about my profession. <u>Offensive</u> means _____.
8. It's so <u>ironic</u>! Keith hates animals, and where does he work? At a zoo! <u>Ironic</u> means _____.
9. I've heard that joke since I was a child! It's <u>ancient</u>! <u>Ancient</u> means _____.

C _____

Listen to the sentences. Write the missing words in the blanks.

1. Does he know that I'm coming?
2. You better ask her your question.
3. We gave him some money.
4. Call his friend right now.
5. What's her name?
6. They told him a joke.

D _____

Read the questions below, and listen to the answers. Identify the answer that goes with each question.

a. In Chicago.
b. At seven o'clock.
c. She's an accountant.
d. A friend.
e. That one.
f. She's fine.

UNIT 8

A

1 *Listen to the interview. Choose the best answer to complete each main idea.*

Interviewer: Abdullah, thanks for speaking with us today.

Abdullah: You're welcome.

Interviewer: Could you describe the traditional clothing in your country?

Abdullah: Well, the men wear a *dishdasha*. It's like a long shirt with long sleeves. For the summer we wear white ones, and for winter we have other colors, like brown and so on. And on our heads we wear a *quitra*, which is a piece of cloth, and an *igal*, which is a piece of rope that you put around your head to keep the *quitra* on.

Interviewer: And do men wear traditional styles a lot?

Abdullah: Yes, I'd say most of the men do.

Interviewer: For both formal and informal occasions?

Abdullah: Sure. It's a way for us to show pride in our culture.

2 *Listen to the interview again. Check the details that are mentioned.*

B

Listen to each sentence and circle the correct answer.

1. When I'm at home, I <u>tend to</u> watch TV rather than read. To <u>tend to</u> do something means _____.
2. Jerome has a <u>unique</u> way of dressing that often surprises his friends. <u>Unique</u> is _____.
3. These old tools don't have much <u>value</u>. You should get rid of them. Something that has <u>value</u> is _____.
4. Marty often <u>hangs out</u> at Jake's Place. He often sees his friends there. To <u>hang out</u> at a place means _____.
5. It's difficult to be <u>in style</u> when you don't have much money to buy clothes. To be <u>in style</u> means _____.
6. When I traveled around the world, I ate some pretty <u>exotic</u> food, such as snake meat. <u>Exotic</u> is _____.
7. In this warm weather, light clothing, such as shorts and a T-shirt, is much more <u>practical</u> than a heavy suit. <u>Practical</u> is _____.
8. My friends' way of dressing seems to have <u>influenced</u> me, because we wear the same kinds of clothes all the time. To <u>influence</u> means _____.
9. I'd much rather go to an old-style restaurant with good food than a <u>trendy</u> restaurant with bad food. <u>Trendy</u> is _____.
10. Cindy's <u>attitude</u> about style has changed a lot in recent years. An <u>attitude</u> is _____.

C

Listen to the sentences. Circle the number of thought groups you hear in each sentence.

1. In Sri Lanka, many older women wear saris.
2. Saris are traditional.
3. They can be very beautiful.
4. However, many younger women don't wear them.
5. They don't wear them, they say, because they're too old-fashioned.
6. They're great for formal wear, but if you're just hanging out, you want something else.

D

*Listen to what each person says. Complete each sentence with **used to** or **didn't use to**.*

1. When I was a teenager, I played tennis a lot. Now I don't.
2. For a while, I loved going to the theater, but I haven't seen a play for a long time.
3. I didn't have e-mail before, but now I use it all the time.
4. I never wore a sari when I was in Sri Lanka. Now I like to wear one.
5. At one time I drank a lot of milk. I stopped drinking it a few years ago.
6. I didn't think much about fashion until I got a job in the fashion industry.

UNIT 9

A

1 *Listen to a mother talk about spanking. Then read the main ideas below. Write **M** to identify the mother's opinions and **F** to identify the father's opinions.*

My husband and I disagree about how to discipline our children. We have different ideas about how to punish them when they misbehave. He thinks spanking is acceptable. He says that we should do it for their own good, so our children will learn right and wrong. He wants our children to respect us and listen to what we say.

I'm against spanking. I admit that I sometimes feel like hitting my children when I'm very angry, but I think it's wrong. Spanking is a form of violence. It is a form of child abuse and is very harmful to children. In my opinion, people who spank their children should be arrested and put in jail. Spanking can lead to more serious problems. When kids get in trouble, we need to talk to them and find out the problem, not spank them.

My husband and I have a lot of arguments about this. He complains that I do not really punish the kids. I think he abuses them.

2 *Listen again and mark the details **T** (true) or **F** (false).*

B

Listen to the people talk about disciplining children. Circle the best word or phrase to complete each opinion.

1. When I spank my children, it's for their own _____.
2. I don't believe in corporal _____.
3. I spank my children because I want them to _____.
4. I prefer to talk with my children when they _____.
5. It's terrible. Sometimes people who spank their children are treated like _____.
6. I don't approve of hitting a child. In my opinion, it's just not _____.
7. Spanking is sometimes a necessary way to _____.
8. I don't spank my kids because it isn't effective. Most people know that, but they won't _____.
9. I think spanking is O.K. If kids know they will be spanked for doing something wrong, they won't _____.
10. Some people agree with spanking, but I don't _____.

C

Listen to the sentences and the words. Circle the word you hear in each sentence.

1. We didn't have any **peace. Peace**
2. They gave us a **raise. Raise**
3. I saw the **plays. Plays**
4. Was it the best **price? Price**
5. Look at her **knees. Knees**
6. We hear the **bus. Bus**

D

Listen to the sentences. Are they in the present perfect or another tense? Check the correct answers in the chart below.

1. Spanking has decreased in the past 50 years.
2. Do you have the statistics about spanking?
3. I've changed my opinion about spanking.
4. He read the report about spanking.
5. Doctors have advised parents not to spank their children.
6. They've suggested using other methods of discipline.

UNIT 10

A

1 *Listen to the excerpt and mark each main idea **T** (true) or **F** (false).*

After we got married, I found out that my husband and I had different expectations about marriage. He wanted me to do all the cleaning, while I thought that we should share it. Before we were married, he lived by himself and cleaned his own apartment. So it bothered me that suddenly, after we were married, he didn't want to do any cleaning!

Fortunately, we were able to work out the problem. We sat down and talked. We both explained our point of view. Then we reached a compromise. We each agreed to cook dinner three times a week. We also divided the cleaning chores in half. We had to spend a lot of time talking, but we finally agreed on something that made us both happy.

2 *Listen again. Circle the best answer to complete the details.*

B

Listen to each sentence and circle the correct answer.

1. Jeff's car is old and has some quirks, but he loves it. A quirk is _____.
2. John and Carol's expectations in marriage were very different, so they got divorced. Expectations are _____.
3. It bothers Sam that he and his wife don't have a prenuptial agreement. To bother means _____.
4. Many couples' arguments concern money. Concern means _____.
5. I don't like to play cards with someone who breaks the rules. To break the rules means _____.
6. When her children go out of town, Emily likes to check on them. To check on someone means _____.
7. Some people think a contract between two married people isn't very romantic. People who are romantic behave like _____.
8. I hope that Adam and Sarah can work out the problems in their marriage. To work out means _____.
9. The Dawsons have a prenuptial agreement, but it isn't legal. Legal means _____.
10. Jess and Donna like different types of food, but they reached a compromise about where to go for dinner. Compromise means _____.

C

Listen to each sentence. Underline the word that is emphasized. Then circle the correct meaning.

1. Karen will take care of meals.
2. We agree to share chores inside the house.
3. We will exercise and eat healthy food.
4. Steve will wash the clothes.
5. On weekdays we will wake up by 6 A.M.
6. We will both make a grocery list.
7. We will spend 15 minutes talking with each other.

D

Listen to each sentence. Circle the correct response.

1. Bob went to a restaurant.
2. Bob gave Janet the present.
3. Bob and Janet had an argument.
4. Bob and Janet are renting the house.
5. Bob went to a friend's wedding.
6. Bob's friend works for the newspaper.

Achievement Tests
Test 1 Answer Key

UNIT 1

A _____

1️⃣ 1. F   2. F   3. T
2️⃣ 1. (blank)   2. (blank)   3. (✓)   4. (✓)

B _____

1. d	4. b	7. e	10. i
2. c	5. h	8. f	11. j
3. a	6. g	9. k	

C _____

1. are	5. on
2. terrible	6. dandruff
3. happened	7. concentrate
4. job	

D _____

1. c, g   2. a, i   3. e, f   4. d, h   5. b, j

UNIT 2

A _____

1️⃣ 1. F   2. T   3. T
2️⃣ 1. (✓)   2. (blank)   3. (✓)   4. (✓)
    5. (blank)

B _____

1. b	6. a
2. a	7. a
3. b	8. b
4. b	9. a
5. b	10. a

C _____

1. b	5. b
2. a	6. b
3. a	7. b
4. b	

D _____

1. a   2. b   3. a   4. a   5. a

UNIT 3

A _____

1️⃣ Correct order: 2, 4, 1, 3
2️⃣ 1. F   2. F   3. F   4. T

B _____

1. a	5. a
2. a	6. a
3. b	7. a
4. b	

C _____

1. a	4. b
2. b	5. a
3. a	

D _____

1. Not reduced	4. Not reduced
2. Reduced	5. Reduced
3. Not reduced	6. Reduced

E _____

1. a   2. b   3. a   4. b

UNIT 4

A _____

1️⃣ 1. T   2. T   3. F
2️⃣ 1. (blank)   2. (✓)   3. (blank)   4. (✓)

B _____

1. b	7. a
2. a	8. a
3. a	9. a
4. a	10. b
5. a	11. a
6. b	12. b

C _____

1. b	4. a
2. b	5. a
3. b	6. a

D _____

1. d   2. a   3. e   4. c   5. b

UNIT 5

A _____

1. 1. T   2. T   3. F
2. 1. (✓)   2. (✓)   3. (blank)   4. (✓)
    5. (blank)   6. (✓)

B _____

1. b   6. a
2. a   7. b
3. a   8. b
4. b   9. b
5. a   10. b

C _____

1. Can   5. can't
2. can't   6. can
3. can't   7. Can't
4. can   8. can

D _____

1. b   2. a   3. b   4. c   5. c

UNIT 6

A _____

1. 1. F   2. T   3. F
2. 1. (blank)   2. (✓)   3. (blank)   4. (✓)
    5. (blank)

B _____

1. a   5. b
2. b   6. b
3. a   7. a
4. a

C _____

1. positive   4. positive
2. negative   5. positive
3. neutral   6. negative

D _____

1. /əd/   4. /t/
2. /t/   5. /t/
3. /d/   6. /əd/

E _____

1. went   4. bought
2. got   5. spent
3. rented

UNIT 7

A _____

1. Correct order: 2, 4, 1, 3
2. 1. (✓)   2. (blank)   3. (blank)   4. (✓)
    5. (✓)

B _____

1. b   6. e
2. a   7. i
3. c   8. h
4. f   9. g
5. d

C _____

1. Does he   4. Call his
2. ask her   5. What's her
3. gave him   6. told him

D _____

1. c   4. d
2. e   5. b
3. f   6. a

UNIT 8

A _____

1. 1. a   2. b
2. 1. (✓)   2. (✓)   3. (blank)   4. (blank)
    5. (✓)   6. (blank)

B _____

1. a   6. a
2. b   7. a
3. a   8. b
4. b   9. b
5. a   10. a

C _____

1. 2   4. 2
2. 1   5. 3
3. 1   6. 3

D _____

1. used to   4. didn't use to
2. used to   5. used to
3. didn't use to   6. didn't use to

UNIT 9

A

1 1. M   2. F   3. F   4. M

2 1. T   2. F   3. T   4. T

B

1. a	6. b
2. b	7. a
3. b	8. a
4. a	9. a
5. b	10. b

C

1. a	4. a
2. b	5. b
3. b	6. a

D

1. Present perfect	4. Another tense
2. Another tense	5. Present perfect
3. Present perfect	6. Present perfect

UNIT 10

A

1 1. T   2. F

2 1. a   2. a   3. b   4. a   5. b

B

1. a	6. b
2. b	7. a
3. b	8. b
4. a	9. a
5. b	10. b

C

1. a	5. b
2. a	6. b
3. a	7. b
4. b	

D

1. a	4. a
2. a	5. b
3. a	6. a

Notes

Notes

Notes

Notes

Notes

CD Tracking Guide
Achievement Tests

TEST 1
1. Audio Program Introduction

UNIT 1
2. A. 1
3. A. 2
4. B.
5. C.
6. D.

UNIT 2
7. A. 1
8. A. 2
9. B.
10. C.
11. D.

UNIT 3
12. A. 1
13. A. 2
14. B.
15. C.
16. D.
17. E.

UNIT 4
18. A. 1
19. A. 2
20. B.
21. C.
22. D.

UNIT 5
23. A. 1
24. A. 2
25. B.
26. C.
27. D.

UNIT 6
28. A. 1
29. A. 2
30. B.
31. C.
32. D.
33. E.

UNIT 7
34. A. 1
35. A. 2
36. B.
37. C.
38. D.

UNIT 8
39. A. 1
40. A. 2
41. B.
42. C.
43. D.

UNIT 9
44. A. 1
45. A. 2
46. B.
47. C.
48. D.

UNIT 10
49. A. 1
50. A. 2
51. B.
52. C.
53. D.